36 Amazing Memory Tricks

Dr. Vinod Sharma

DIAMOND BOOKS
www.diamondbooks.in

Publisher	**:**	**Diamond Pocket Books (P) Ltd.** X-30, Okhla Industrial Area, Phase-II, New Delhi-110020
Phone	:	011-40712200
E-mail	:	wecare@diamondbooks.in
Website	:	www.diamondbooks.in
Edition	:	2025
Printed By	:	Repro (India)

---

36 Amazing Memory Tricks

Author - *Dr. Vinod Sharma*

***With blessings of MAA SARASWATI,
I dedicate this book to my parents, my wife
Megha and my son Ayaan.***

*Many thanks and regards to
our ideal, Chairman of Diamond Books-
Shri Narender Kumar Verma Sir for his
valuable guidance and motivation in
writing of this book.*

Many thanks to
Mrs Alka Dhal for her great support in translation and editing of this book.

Special thanks to
Mr Dhruv Suwalka, Mr Rajnish Suwalka and whole Brainywood family for their constant motivation, support and blessings.

Author's Note

If there's a question in front of you about whether we want our child to be educated and successful, the natural answer is yes, we want them to be successful. We also want them to be educated so they can achieve success.

Do you agree that there are many people who may not have scored well in exams or completed their education, yet they are successful and prosperous in their lives? Similarly, there are also many who have studied a lot, earned good grades and degrees, but are still striving for their desired success.

So, scoring good marks and completing education is indeed an important milestone in the journey of success, but it's not the only definition of success. "Just getting good grades in exams is not the destination."

"Today, you failed again, you always get such low marks. It seems your mind is very weak. You'll never be successful in life like this," the teacher scolded the child. Because once again, he had scored low marks in the exam, and eventually, he failed in the annual exam. The teacher even made a terrifying prediction to his mother, *"This child won't be able to do anything in the future."* These words started spinning in the mother's mind, and she became very worried. However, this statement had a different effect on the child's mind, and he grew up. One day, he told his mother, "This child won't be able to do anything in the future," and saying this, he placed India's highest civilian honor - the Bharat Ratna, in his mother's hands, which he had received. Tears of love and pride flowed from the mother's eyes, and with tears of joy and pride, the Bharat Ratna was adorned, and the mother embraced the boy.

And that boy was none other than the great cricketer Sachin Tendulkar. Sachin Tendulkar, Dhirubhai Ambani, Bill Gates, Amitabh Bachchan, and many others are examples of individuals who may not have excelled greatly in their studies and exams, yet their definition of success is an inspiration for millions of people and a matter of pride for the entire nation.

Scoring well in exams is important, but it's not the sole destination in life. The purpose of education is to make one capable. It's not just about scoring high marks.

Practice makes perfect - practice turns everything into a child's play.

Turning everything into a child's play means, it becomes very easy. That is, less effort yields greater results.

No task is inherently difficult or easy. It becomes easy if there is mastery, meaning perfection, and difficult if there is no perfection. Any task is always difficult in the beginning, then it requires more attention, even with more focus and hard work, results are still less. And when it is done continuously, gradually the mind becomes proficient in that task, and when there is good practice of that task, it becomes your skill. And then with less effort, there are quicker and more accurate results in that task.

Like when learning to ride a bicycle, despite falling repeatedly even with more attention and more effort, balance is not achieved even with more focus, but with continuous practice, proficiency in riding the bicycle is acquired. And it starts to feel very easy to ride it. Similarly, whether it's using a computer, cooking, playing a sport, or studying, it's practice that can turn a difficult task into an easy one, meaning it becomes child's play.

A player becomes a champion not just by knowing the game well, but by practicing it extensively. Milkha Singh, Sachin Tendulkar, Muhammad Ali, Roger Federer, and all champions in their respective fields have become great through practice. Without practice, even the talent of a talented person becomes inactive and deteriorates. No matter how good the voice is, to become a good singer, one has to practice diligently. Lata Mangeshkar, Kishore Kumar, Sonu Nigam are good singers not just because of their voices but also because of their rigorous practice. The bigger the artist, the more they practice. Expert actors like Amitabh Bachchan, Shah Rukh Khan, Salman Khan, and Aamir Khan or anyone else, don't just start delivering dialogues perfectly from the start, but they keep practicing to refine their acting skills. Sachin, Virat Kohli, Dhoni all know how to play cricket well, yet they practice on the field every day.

To be successful, one must work hard, and to stay at the pinnacle of success, one must practice. Practice should be considered a habit, as it has no end; it is something that must be done throughout life to excel in any task.

What a beautiful saying:

"To meet eye to eye is remarkable,
To dissolve in each other's breath is extraordinary.
Reaching heights is not remarkable,
Staying at the top is remarkable."

The law of attraction states that if you truly desire something from the heart, the entire universe conspires to make it happen for you. When you tune a radio, a song starts playing, where is that song? Is it in the radio or in the environment? We all know it's in the environment.

It's invisible, but when the radio aligns its frequency with it, the song becomes available to the radio. Similarly, if we align ourselves with dedication and focus towards our goals, we will surely achieve them. Swami Vivekananda also said, *"First think, then believe in that thought, and align that thought with your mind, intellect, soul, and entire personality."*

Just make that thought your identity, think about it all the time, act according to it, and then see, nobody can stop you from being successful. Not only will you be successful, but you'll also become an inspiration to the world. It depends on how you want to achieve your goals or your dreams. That's why Kalam Sahab also said, *"Dreams are not what you see in your sleep, rather dreams are those which do not let you sleep."*

Arastu once asked Socrates, "What is the exact way to achieve a goal?"

Socrates replied, "When I go to the pond to bathe today, come there, and you will find the answer to this question." Arastu was surprised, and his curiosity led him to the pond. Socrates was in the pond, and he told Arastu, "If you want to see the path to your goal, come into the pond." When Arastu entered the pond, Socrates grabbed his head and dunked him into the water. After struggling for a while, Socrates pulled him out of the water. Arastu took a deep breath, coughed, and asked about the reason for this strange behaviour. He thought his guru was angry with him for some reason and had punished him.

Socrates smiled and said, "When you were underwater, what did you feel the need for the most? The breath of air." He felt that if he couldn't breathe, he would die. "Did you think of anything else to attain?" Socrates asked. Arastu replied, "No, Guruji, I only had one thought and made only one effort—to get air no matter what." Socrates said, "That's the path to achieving your goal. When the only thought is to attain the goal, and when nothing is visible but still, you strive to achieve it, that's the mindset needed to attain the goal."

When Guru Dronacharya was teaching archery to his disciples, he set the goal of hitting the eye of a bird on a tree. As the disciples aimed and hit the target, he asked them what they saw besides the bird's eye. Some said the tree, some said the bird, but the most skilled disciple, Arjuna, said, "I only see the bird's eye, nothing else." Hence, Arjuna became the greatest and most skilled archer.

Let's embark on this journey of strengthening and sharpening the mind through neuroscience, making it powerful and intelligent, which makes it easier to achieve success in academics and life.

Yours,

Dr. Vinod Sharma

9672999903, 7665500321

Contents

Kaash (wish)

Who fears war? Only those who don't know how to fight. A warrior doesn't fear; instead, they prepare to demonstrate their skill in battle. Fear arises in the pursuit lacking knowledge and skill. As knowledge and skill grow, fear diminishes.

Have you watched the movies 'Baahubali', 'Sultan', or 'Dangal'? In all these films, I learned one thing: the protagonists were skilled warriors who weren't afraid of fighting. Instead, they aimed to win. It's simple - the weak are afraid, and the strong aren't. This strength doesn't come just from thinking but requires ample learning and practice."

In these movies, all the heroes also worked hard to develop their skills. No task is easy or difficult, it is made easy from difficult. To make any task easy, one has to be skilled in it. To succeed, you have to be at the forefront by participating in competition. Remember, competition is not between the incompetent and the competent, but between the competent and the skilled. In the field of studies, your exam is a battle, and to win this battle, your mind has to become a warrior. A weak mind will fear the exam battle, while a strong and prepared mind will conquer it.

Let's find out how to become capable and adept at studying and facing exams.

The "KASH" Formula - The Sure Formula for Success - K, A, S, and H.

In any exam, whether it's studying or life, a word often comes to mind: "Kash!! Kash!! Kash!!" This "Kash" symbolizes regret. If we look at this regret from another perspective today, we'll never have to say "Kash" in life again. This "Kash" is made up of four letters in the English language - K, A, S, and H. K stands for Knowledge, A stands for Attitude, S stands for Skills, and H stands for Habit. The "KASH" formula can make you a successful student.

K - Knowledge: Knowledge is the first necessity for any task. Recognition of any successful individual in the world is based on their knowledge in their field of work.

Any desire is not fulfilled just by wishing; one must acquire complete knowledge about it. For example, if someone is sick and needs an operation. No matter how positively we think that we need to fix him, we need to save him, we cannot perform his operation ourselves because we don't know how to do it. If we do it without knowledge, the patient won't get better. Your intentions are good - you want to save him. But your knowledge is not sufficient. So, having accurate and adequate knowledge is the foremost and fundamental requirement for success.

A - Attitude or behaviour, human behaviour or perspective is its main component, which determines its success and failure. In reality, your reactions are determined by the circumstances. Negative thinking or a negative attitude can never lead to positive or successful outcomes. On the other hand, a positive attitude, i.e., a positive behaviour, not only leads to success naturally but can also make the impossible possible. Attitude shapes your dreams and transforms thoughts into resolutions. It distinguishes between desire and determination. There's a significant difference between desire and determination; desire can be traded, alternatives can be considered, but determination cannot be traded. It has no room for alternatives. And whenever pressure mounts, desire weakens in life, and determination becomes stronger. Where many ordinary players leave the field under pressure, the winner makes history and becomes a world champion. Strong resolve and positive attitude make this possible. Pressure and stress also depend on your attitude in studies. If you prepare for exams with a positive mindset and determination to excel in any situation, no one can stop you from succeeding in them.

S - Skill or Expertise, Knowledge is necessary to do any work. But to reach the highest position in that work and to establish recognition, it is very important to be skilled in it. Skill comes from continuous practice of knowledge. Along with that, firm determination gives you the ability to face and overcome challenges. When I also decided to learn cooking like my mother, after acquiring the complete knowledge of cooking on the first day, with the belief that I too can now cook well, I went to the kitchen, tried to cook, and then I experienced that despite having the knowledge of cooking, I couldn't cook as well as my mother.

It took me a long time, yet the food didn't turn out well, whereas my mother prepares the entire household meal in just a shortwhile and that is delicious too. The reason for this was that the knowledge was equal in both cases, but my mother had more skill. When learning to drive, one gains knowledge of its technical aspects on the very first day. However, the skill of driving comes with continuous practice. Only then can one easily drive the car correctly. This applies to the field as well. In studies too, along with knowledge, skill shows the path to success.

H - Habit or addiction, Habit helps in transforming knowledge into skill. Unsuccessful people don't like to work hard. Their mind also needs relaxation. But successful people, even if they don't like hard work and fatigue, still do it. And by doing it consistently, it becomes their habit. Those who score low marks do not like studying and prefer playing more. Similarly, students who score well in exams also prefer playing and relaxing more than studying. However, due to the commitment to scoring well, they make studying hard work their habit. Whether a habit is good or bad, it forms by consistently doing that task. Even if laziness comes in going for a morning walk, going for a walk consistently makes it a habit. Once it becomes a habit, doing that task feels easy. To form a habit, one should do that task continuously for twenty-one days, then it becomes a habit in the mind, and skill in that work develops. Yes, in these twenty-one days, one day should not be missed from that task. If there are topics or questions in studies that seem difficult and bother you, if you do them every day for twenty-one days, they will start to seem easy.

❐

10 Habits that can make you a successful student

1. Positive Thinking - Always think about how to be successful and stay positive. No matter what the subject or exam is, don't be afraid, nor stressed. Instead, tell yourself that your mind and determination can overcome anything. Never think it's difficult, say it's easy, I can definitely do it. Don't stress, see problems not as problems but as puzzles or challenges. Solving puzzles or challenges is enjoyable. If you have this kind of thinking, life's problems will be solved, and you will find joy in solving them.

2. Time Management - Organize and manage your activities and tasks systematically. Divide your time into segments and plan your daily routine accordingly. Divide time into urgent and important categories and prioritize your tasks accordingly. Keep tasks that are important but not urgent on a secondary level, and give priority to tasks that are urgent. For example, if your electricity bill has arrived at home, and the due date is fifteen days away, it is important but not urgent. However, on the day of the due date, the task becomes not only important but also urgent.

3. Effective Study Habits - Study not just to score marks, but also to learn and acquire knowledge. Develop an emotional connection with the subjects. Generate interest in them. Learn not only as a subject but also as a skill for life. Just as we use

Facebook, the internet, and WhatsApp not just to score marks but for knowledge and out of interest. Similarly, we read newspapers not just to score marks but to stay informed and updated with current information. Similarly, with our subjects, focus on understanding the essence of the topic along with its relevance in life.

4. Study with intervals - Just as we cannot eat all our meals at once throughout the day and need to eat at different intervals, similarly, instead of continuous studying, take a break of ten to fifteen minutes after every hour of study. Relax. This helps in consolidation of learning and gives the brain a replenishment of energy.

5. Good Sleep - Good and sufficient sleep keeps your mind organized and energetic. Get a full eight hours of sleep; don't stay awake at night to study. Instead, manage your syllabus time according to your schedule and study during the day. Only sleep at night.

6. Be Innovative - Always think of doing something new, keep acquiring new knowledge about a subject. Stay Curious - Keep being inquisitive.

7. Good Nutrition - Always eat good and healthy food. Avoid eating too much fast food and food from the market. Consume salads, fruits, and fruit juices. Drink plenty of water, as it keeps your body and mind fresh and healthy.

8. Focus and Exercise - Students should keep both their mind and body healthy. They should engage in regular exercise and meditation. This helps in keeping the mind and body healthy, energetic, and powerful. It enhances concentration.

9. Organize for Exams - Ensure timely preparation of important questions and topics. Where there is confusion, seek help from teachers to understand them again. Set goals for how much syllabus needs to be covered and how many marks need to be obtained.

10. Focus on One Thing at a Time - Instead of studying everything at once, focus on one question or subject at a time. This is the curriculum. Think about which questions will come and whether they will be correct.

❐

Eight Traits of Good & Wise Parents

1. Trust - Have faith in your child's abilities and earn their trust. Every child has the potential to succeed; their methods might just differ. Your bond with your child should be so strong that they feel comfortable sharing every aspect of their life with you without hiding anything. This trust is built through actions, not just words.

2. Be a Good Listener - Listen to your child attentively and completely. Understand them emotionally and analytically before drawing conclusions. If they make a mistake, allow them to explain their side before scolding or blaming them.

3. Spend Time with Your Children - In today's busy world, many parents struggle to find time for their children, even though they know their child is the most precious thing in their lives. Often, parents provide for their child's daily needs and get them into good schools but fail to spend quality time with them. Remember, along with fulfilling their needs, your personal presence and time are fundamental necessities for your child. Spend time with them, listen to them, and talk with them.

4. Motivate Your Children - Encourage your child to engage in any task, whether it is studying or any other work, through motivation rather than fear or pressure. When motivated, the mind connects with the task, whereas pressure makes it avoid the task. Focus on the benefits of successfully completing the work instead of the consequences of not doing it, and inspire them accordingly.

5. Don't Teach Just for Grades - Don't pressurize your child to study solely for the sake of grades and exams. Instead, motivate them to study with the understanding that the true purpose of education is the holistic development of their personality. Recognize their strengths related to their studies and understand their challenges.

6. Provide Healthy and Nutritious Food - Avoid letting your children develop the habit of eating anything from the market. Remember, a healthy body and a healthy mind are both essential for children. Instead of packaged and fast food, prepare and serve delicious and nutritious meals at home.

7. Be Their Friend - Many things in a child's life can influence them, both positively and negatively. Always be a true and good friend to understand and guide your child's life.

8. Encourage Their Strengths - Identify and encourage your child's unique strengths. If they sing well, excel in a sport, or have any other special talent, do not overlook it. Instead, encourage them wholeheartedly. Remember, it is these very strengths that make us know figures like Sachin Tendulkar, Amitabh Bachchan, A.P.J. Abdul Kalam, and Sania Mirza. Praise what your child is good at, and as a friend, help them overcome any weaknesses. Understand what your child's goals in life might be, or in which area they want to succeed, rather than imposing your own goals on them.

❐

(1)

Visualized Association

Memory in the brain is the combination of two pieces of information; this is what we call association. If we use this association methodically, we can remember everything we want to remember. The importance of remembering anything lies in being able to recall it at the right time. To recall any information, a question is needed. Notice that to remember anything stored in your memory, we ask a related question. In exams, questions are asked, which include a part of any information, and the related information is written in the answers.

The ability to remember well and completely depends on how the information is combined. If we can somehow link pieces of information so that one piece helps recall the other, we will be able to remember most things.

❒

2

Concentration and interest

My sister came to me and said, "Vinod, you teach advanced mind techniques, do something for your nephew too." I asked, "What happened?" She replied, "His concentration is weak, he doesn't focus on his studies." I observed that when my nephew sat down to study, he would close himself in a quiet room. During exams, he would impose a curfew on the whole house: "Dad, don't make any noise. Sister, don't play songs. Uncle, turn off the TV volume. I have exams and I can't concentrate with so much noise." I thought that concentration required solitude and silence, and that any external noise would disrupt focus.

This is why all of us, when we study or memorize something, prefer to do it in a quiet, noise-free environment.

So, I thought that to concentrate and focus, one needed a quiet, solitary place without any noise or disturbances. However, this notion proved to be wrong when I saw my nephew watching cartoons on TV. While he was watching cartoons, his mother called him several times, "Gaurang, come here, eat your food." She even yelled into his ear, but he did not budge, as if he hadn't heard her at all; he was completely engrossed in watching his cartoon. This means that his full attention was focused on watching the cartoon. At that moment, I understood that when things or information are interesting, our mind automatically gets absorbed in them, and concentration becomes complete. This means that concentration is not inherently weak or strong, but it is directed by interest and curiosity. Additionally, I conducted another experiment: I asked Gaurang several questions related to the cartoon, and he gave precise answers to all of them. He remembered everything, even the old episodes. You could ask him anything, and he would know it as if he had memorized and reviewed it hundreds of times, even though he had only watched the cartoon once. This made me realize that if a subject is interesting, the mind naturally gets engaged, and remembering also becomes effortless.

We should make subjects and study information interesting to study. To make studying interesting, mnemonic techniques, associations, and imagination can be used. In the upcoming sections, I will describe some methods that can make studying more interesting and engaging. Concentration is neither weak nor strong but rather directed by interest and engagement. Along with this, I conducted another experiment. I asked Gaurang several questions related to that cartoon, and he answered all of them accurately. He remembered everything, even the old episodes, and could answer anything as if he had memorized and repeated it hundreds of times, even though he had only watched the cartoon once. This made me realize that if a subject is interesting, the mind automatically becomes engaged, and remembering also happens naturally. We should make subjects and study information interesting to study. To make studying interesting, mnemonic techniques, associations, and imagination can be used. In the upcoming sections, I will describe some methods that can make studying more interesting and engaging.

❐

3

Creative Imagination

Have you ever seen a dog talking on a mobile phone? Or a goat going to a beauty parlour, or a donkey taking math tuition? Reading this might make you laugh, and it probably seems strange. You might be wondering what kind of things Mr. Vinod is talking about today. But the point to understand here is that all these activities happen around us all the time. We humans do these things regularly, and it doesn't surprise us because, for us, it's normal. However, animals or other creatures can't do these things. But you must know that millions of years ago, these animals and we were the same. We lived similar lives, in forests and caves. The primary task for everyone was finding food, and after obtaining food, returning to their place. But we humans have changed. We have created so much, invented so much, and changed the entire map of the world. From forests to cities and from caves to luxurious buildings, humans have made this journey using the power of their minds. But do you know which power of the brain enables a person to do this? It is creative imagination.

Nature has endowed every creature with some unique physical characteristic that, in some way, is more distinct and powerful than the physical strength given to humans. For example, a lion has sharp teeth and claws, an elephant has immense strength, a bird can fly, and a fish can swim underwater. Animals have these physical traits, whereas humans do not possess such physical features. Despite this, humans dominate the world on a much larger scale than these animals and even keep animals under their control. The reason for this is the greatest trait of humans: their brain. This trait makes humans powerful beings. But do you know what gives the brain this power? It is creative imagination. That means the human brain can imagine with creativity. In other words, a person can imagine what they have not seen and think about creating it. It is through this power that so many inventions and changes have occurred. Science is also a form of creative imagination. Any change, discovery, or invention is initially just an imagination, and the creativity of the mind gives it form and possibility. An amazing fact is that imagination is not influenced by logic. Imagination comes first, and logic provides the foundation later. For example, imagine there is a lion sitting on your sofa eating chocolate. As soon as you start imagining it, you can see this scene in your mind—a lion eating chocolate appears vividly. Logically, we know that lions do not eat chocolate. Let's take another example: do not think about a red apple. See, despite my instruction, the image of a red apple appeared in your mind. This means that imagination is faster and unaffected by logic. Albert Einstein also said that a person's imagination is the most powerful thing in the world. We just need to learn how to use this power in our studies and in any task, we undertake in life. This is what makes the impossible possible.

❐

4

Brain Science and the Phonics Method

Everyone knows the importance of memorization for exams. But do you know that the time required to remember information varies according to the type of information and subject matter? Have you ever noticed how much time it actually takes to memorize something? Often, we don't know how much time is needed to fully and thoroughly memorize a particular subject or chapter. In fact, the time required for memorization depends on the type of subject or information.

The easiest things to remember are those that can be seen, which form a three-dimensional image, like the objects shown to young children in play school, which they learn by observing. More difficult than this is remembering words. Even more challenging is remembering rhyming content like poems. Harder than that is remembering groups of sentences or theory. The most difficult of all is remembering numbers because they are abstract.

In reality, the brain finds it easier and quicker to remember information that has both a literal meaning and a visual cue. For example, if I say "aeroplane," an image of an aeroplane appears in your mind, along with the word and its meaning. When both a word and an image accompany information, these are auxiliary cues that aid in memorization. These cues make the subject simpler. However, if I say "thirty-two," the number

32 will appear in your mind, but no specific image will come to mind. Since numerical information lacks an accompanying visual cue, numerical information can be confusing. And they are memorized only after repeated practice over time. Let's consider how to give numerical information a visual form. If I ask you if you remember your father's first car, you will likely visualize the car. But if I ask you if you remember its license plate number, many people often get confused. When asked which bank you have an account with, your mind will visualize the bank, but you may not remember the account number. Friends' names, addresses, and faces are often remembered, but their phone or mobile numbers need to be noted down in a phone or diary. In studies, square roots, cube roots, mathematical formulas, historical dates, and multiplication tables are often forgotten despite repeated practice. The reason is that the brain takes longer to memorize numerical information and forgets it quickly. Remembering numbers is difficult because they are abstract. In the brain's perspective, information that also presents a visual cue along with its literal meaning is easier and quicker to remember. Numbers lack these visual aids. So today, let's learn how to convert numbers into visual forms.

Brain Science and the Phonics Method

Consider the digits from zero to nine, which form all numbers. Let's convert them into sounds represented by English letters. Assign 'S' to zero, 'T' to one, 'N' to two, 'M' to three, 'R' to four, 'L' to five, 'J' to six, 'K' to seven, 'F' to eight, and 'P' to nine. Note that all the letters assigned to these digits are consonants, not vowels. We will use vowels to create words and images from these letters. Now, let's take an example. To visualize the number twenty-five (2 and 5), use the letters corresponding to these digits: N for two and L for five. By placing a vowel between N and L, we can form a word.

In this way, you can create your own phonetic codes for each number and link these images to the main information for easier recall. For instance, to remember Article 19 of the Constitution, which pertains to "freedom of speech," you can use the number nineteen (1 and 9). The phonetic code for 1 is T and for 9 is P. By adding a vowel, you can form the word "tap" (नल). Imagine holding a tap like a microphone and saying whatever you want, symbolizing freedom of speech. This way, it will be easier to remember.

This method allows numerical information to be transformed into simple visual images.

❐

⑤

VIBGYOR Method

Does the VIBGYOR method ring any bells for you? Let me give you a hint: it is a colourful term. In English, it is called VIBGYOR. Perhaps now most people remember it, as almost all schools teach this word at some point. Let's understand it once again.

When I was a child, my teacher taught me a word to remember the seven colours of the rainbow in order, using the first letter of each colour. That word was VIBGYOR.

Did you know that VIBGYOR is also a mnemonic method? In this method, we use these colours as base or auxiliary information to remember a fact or information. The order of the colors can be used to remember the sequence of events, information, or facts. This method can help in recalling sequences or timelines effectively.

For instance, we can use the colors of VIBGYOR to remember historical centuries. We can associate events from the fourteenth century with the colour violet, events from the fifteenth century with the colour indigo, the sixteenth century with blue, and the seventeenth century with green. For example, we can associate the eighteenth century with yellow, the nineteenth century with orange, and the twentieth century with red. This means that to remember events related to these centuries, we can colour-code the event or fact with the century›s colour. For instance, the construction of the Taj Mahal began in the sixteenth century. To remember this, the colour for the sixteenth century in VIBGYOR is blue. Now, imagine the Taj Mahal is blue, or imagine yourself painting the Taj Mahal blue. In reality, the Taj Mahal is white, but in your imagination, it appears blue, reminding you that it was constructed in the sixteenth century. Another example is Akbar, who is associated with the fifteenth century. Imagine Akbar's clothes, his palace, and his elephants and horses all in indigo, because indigo represents the fifteenth century in the VIBGYOR sequence. Whenever you need to recall a fact about Akbar, visualize it in indigo, which will always remind you of his century.

Now, remember logically that we are memorizing centuries numerically here. We should know that in numbers, the twentieth century is called the twenty first century. The reason is that when the first century was numbered, it was called the first century according to the Gregorian calendar, not the zero century. This made the first century the second century, and the second century the third. Hence, it is easier to remember the main century in numerical form, and VIBGYOR can be a fun and effective way to remember it. Similarly, if we need to remember long theoretical answers, we can use the order of these colors. For example, if you have a four-page answer to remember, you can make it easier by color-coding each page with a VIBGYOR colour. You can remember the information on the first page in violet, the second page in indigo, the third page in blue, and the fourth page in green. This way, you can remember long descriptive answers. In future sections, we will look at some detailed examples of this.

❑

6

Imaginary Journey, Real Experience: The Seven Wonders Experiment

How do you travel from one city to another today? By bus, car, train, or on foot? If you cover a distance of one hundred kilometers by car, it will take two hours. And if you walk, it will take two days. The distance remains the same, but how you travel affects the time it takes. Five hundred years ago, people travelled on foot, but today we use buses, trains, cars, and airplanes. This has significantly reduced travel time, thanks to science. Science reduces the time, effort, and fatigue required for tasks, making them easier and faster. However, if studying requires more time and effort to achieve good grades, it indicates that while we study science, we do not apply it to our studies.

Just as there are different methods for traveling a certain distance—walking, cycling, taking a bus, train, car, or airplane—each method affects the time and speed of travel differently. Similarly, the time and effort required for studying and memorizing can vary depending on the methods used. Adopting efficient methods can change and save the time and effort needed for studying.

Imaginary Journey, Real Experience: The Seven Wonders Experiment

When we travel with family or friends, we tend to remember almost everything about the trip because the experience is real.

Similarly, we can create an imaginary journey and remember it as if it were a real experience. You may have heard or read about the New Seven Wonders of the World. But do you remember all seven in order? Let's memorize them today. The New Seven Wonders are: Christ the Redeemer in Brazil, the Great Wall of China, Machu Picchu in Peru, Petra in Jordan, Chechen Itza in Mexico, the Colosseum in Rome, and the Taj Mahal in India. One way to remember them is through repetition—repeating the information over and over. However, let's try a different method by imagining a journey where you visit these wonders with your family, creating a memorable experience. Imagine you first travel to Brazil, where you see the enormous statue of Christ the Redeemer. Behind this statue, there's a massive wall stretching all the way to China. You climb this wall and see a match taking place on the other side, where players are levelling the pitch with their feet. Suddenly, someone spills petrol, and a huge fire breaks out. You quickly run to a nearby restaurant and have a Mexican chicken pizza, which turns out to be bad, making you feel sick. You rush to brush your teeth with Colgate, and as you step out of the room, you see the Taj Mahal in front of you. Finally, you return home.

Now, these wonders are firmly situated in your mind as a real experience through this imaginary journey. Don't believe it? Ask yourself where you first went on this journey. Your mind will show you Brazil, where you saw Christ the Redeemer. What was behind it? You'll remember the Great Wall of China. And on the other side of the wall, you'll see the match pitch, representing Machu Picchu. This way, you'll recall all of them. This method allows you to create a vivid, memorable association with each wonder, making it easier to remember them in order.

❒

(7)

A to Z Memory

Today, we will discuss what is essential to make our memory powerful. A strong memory has certain characteristics. Just like how using an adhesive substance helps bind two objects together strongly, adding specific features to information can make it a strong and lasting memory. For example, cement is used to bond bricks and stones together securely. Similarly, by incorporating certain features into the information you want to remember, you can create a strong and permanent memory.

If the following characteristics are added to the information you want to remember, that memory can become strong and permanent:

A = Action: The brain quickly and firmly remembers active information.

B = Big: The brain remembers information that is large in size or impact better.

C = Colourful: Colourful things and information are remembered more strongly.

D = Dimensional: Information that the brain can see in three dimensions is remembered more easily.

E = Emotional: Information that has an emotional impact on the brain is remembered permanently.

F = Feeling: Information that can be felt or experienced is remembered more firmly by the brain.

***G = Game*:** Information received in the form of a game is remembered more easily and quickly.

***H = Happy*:** Information remembered with happiness is recalled better.

***I = Interest*:** Information linked to your interests is easily remembered by the brain.

***J = Joke (Humour)*:** Information that makes you laugh or is humorous is quickly remembered by the brain.

***K = Knowledge*:** Having a thorough understanding of a subject makes it easier to remember related information.

***L = Logical*:** Logical information is remembered more permanently.

***M = Mnemonic*:** Using mnemonic devices can strengthen and firmly establish any information.

***N = Neurobics*:** Just like aerobics is exercise for the body, neurobics is exercise for the brain, using imagination to keep the brain healthy and powerful.

***O = Observation*:** Good observation skills solidify information.

***P = Picture*:** Information presented in the form of pictures is remembered faster and stronger.

***Q = Question*:** Asking questions keeps the brain active and helps in converting information into memory.

***R = Ridiculous*:** Strange thoughts and uniqueness make information easy to remember.

***T = Tuning*:** The brain quickly remembers a tune.

***U = Used To*:** Information that is used regularly is remembered.

***V = Visualization*:** Information that can be visualized in the brain forms a permanent memory.

***W = Water*:** Drinking plenty of water improves memory.

***X = Xerox*:** The brain easily remembers similar-sounding words.

***Y = Yes*:** Saying "yes" to yourself with full positivity helps in quick recall.

***Z = Zeal*:** Doing any task with zeal ensures that the information is firmly remembered.

By using these features, information can be transformed into permanent memories.

❐

8

Imaginative Association

If you have the world's best computer but its hard drive is empty, without any data, it won't be of any use to you. To make it useful, you'll need to load data, or memories, into it. Similarly, everything you know, all your knowledge, and every bit of information in your brain exists in the form of memories. In other words, the brain is a repository of memories. If things in your home are kept in a disorganized or haphazard manner, you won't be able to find them when you need them. However, if they are placed in the right spots, you will find them easily.

Just as you might think you've lost something if you can't find it in your house on time, the reality is that the item is still there, just misplaced—placed somewhere you don't remember. To avoid the problem of misplacing things, you need to designate specific places for everything in your home. When items are kept in their designated spots, they don't get lost. Similarly, to keep memories in the right place within the 'house' of your brain, you can use imaginative and creative associations.

Imaginative Creative Association: Association means a connection, a bond that links two things together. When two things are linked, you only need to remember one of them as long as they are connected. If the items are separate, you need to remember both independently. If there is an association between them, remembering one will automatically bring the other to mind. Creative imagination in the brain provides the basis for this association.

Let's take an example from world geography. Some countries are known for being sources of certain minerals and metals. For instance, copper is most abundantly found in Chile, bauxite is primarily produced in Australia, Russia leads in diamond production, China is known for iron ore, and South Africa is a major producer of platinum and manganese. To make this information a permanent memory, instead of rote memorization and repetition, we can use imaginative associations.

For instance, to remember the connection between copper and Chile, visualize copper wires wrapped around a chili pepper. For bauxite and Australia, create imaginary symbols: bauxite as a boxing glove and Australia as a kangaroo. Now, imagine a kangaroo wearing boxing gloves and boxing in a ring.

For diamond and Russia, diamonds are already a clear image. For Russia, you can imagine a rope (as it sounds like "Russia" in Hindi). Picture a rope in your hand adorned with diamonds. To remember iron ore and China, think of iron as a metal and sugar as a symbol for China. Imagine a large iron container in your house filled with sugar.

For platinum and manganese, you can create imaginary symbols too. For example, you could visualize a platinum ring and manganese as a magnifying glass. Imagine using a magnifying glass to closely inspect a platinum ring.

Using such imaginative and creative associations helps transform information into strong and permanent memories.

For platinum and manganese, if you need to remember that they are found in South Africa, imagine that guests from South Africa have come to your house. You've given them a plate to eat from and a magazine to read. This way, using creative and imaginative associations, these pieces of information get linked together and stay in your memory.

❒

9

The RRR Principle Receiving, Retention & Recollection

Everyone wants to remember things quickly and never forget them. It's frustrating when you can't recall something despite repeated attempts. Students often ask me what they should do to remember things quickly. However, the real issue is not how to remember quickly, but how to remember in a way that makes recall easy during exams. The hallmark of a permanent memory is not just how quickly you remember it, but how easily you can recall it when needed. Sometimes, one piece of information is linked to many others, creating confusion.

For instance, wheat is produced in Uttar Pradesh, but it is also grown in Punjab and Haryana. Similarly, sugarcane is grown in Uttar Pradesh and Maharashtra. These multiple associations can create confusion. Let's understand how to make such information permanent memory.

The RRR Principle: Receiving, Retention, and Recollection.

The association of information is called memory, and the mutual association of memories creates permanent memory. There are two types of memory: temporary and permanent. Permanent memory is something you always remember and can recall instantly. We constantly receive information in various forms, but most of it becomes temporary memory. To make a memory permanent, we need to understand the RRR principle.

These are the stages of turning information into memory and using it:

1. ***Receiving*:** The first 'R' stands for Receiving, which means acquiring the information.
2. ***Retention*:** The second 'R' stands for Retention, which means storing the information.
3. ***Recollection*:** The third 'R' stands for Recollection, which means retrieving the information.

We can think of these stages as remembering, storing, and recalling. This can also be called remembering, retaining, and recalling. The most crucial among these is recollection. However, the foundation for recollection is retention. Therefore, our primary focus should be on retention. Just like how items in a house might not be found on time even though they were brought into the house, they were not placed in the right spot. So, finding them on time depends on keeping them in the right place.

If you need to place new clothes in a wardrobe, and it is already filled with old clothes, what will you do? You will first remove the old clothes to make space for the new ones. In today's world, most people have tension in their minds, which is why essential memories do not become permanent. The mind should have retention, not tension. To utilize retention effectively, one should use imagination and association. For example, if sugarcane is produced in both Uttar Pradesh (UP) and Maharashtra, to remember this, you can create an imaginative picture associating both states with sugarcane. UP's symbol could be the Taj Mahal, and Maharashtra's could be Bollywood (cinema). Now you can imagine yourself drinking sugarcane juice while watching a movie about the Taj Mahal in a cinema. Similarly, to remember the wheat-producing states, imagine the Taj Mahal surrounded by lush greenery (Haryana) where many people are happily harvesting wheat and dancing Bhangra (Punjab). Now, you have placed the information in the right spot in your mind using imaginative pictures and connected them together. So, if you are asked about any of these pieces of information, the rest will automatically come to mind. Because recollection is based on retention.

❐

10

Imaginative Abbreviation Method

Have you ever noticed that people don't praise you for remembering something, but for recalling it? In other words, nobody cares about how long it took you to memorize something; they care about how quickly you can recall it. Even in exams, marks are given for recall, not for memorization. Memorizing is the input, and recalling is the output, and the world values the output. But it's true that recalling depends on memorizing—how well you memorize something will determine how accurately you can recall it. In other words, a precise output relies on precise input.

Sometimes, we need to remember abbreviations, and it can be confusing to recall what each letter stands for. If we assign imaginative meanings to the letters in the abbreviation, we can remember them without much repetition and confusion.

Imaginative Abbreviation Method

The imaginative abbreviation method involves creating a short form of a long name or a name with multiple words by combining the first letters of the words to form an abbreviation. This abbreviation is then remembered as a symbolic name. For example, the full form of "S.A.I" is "Sports Authority of India," and "D.I.A" stands for "Defence Intelligence Agency," commonly known as D.I.A. "P.O.T.A" is short for "Prevention of Terrorism Act." Instead of repeatedly memorizing such information, it can be remembered using the imaginative abbreviation method. Here, we create an image based on the abbreviation and connect it with the main idea of the full form. Let's try it out:

1. S.A.I (Sports Authority of India) - We can create an imaginative image for "SAI" by thinking of Sai Baba's temple. Now, connect this with the main idea of sports by imagining people praying at Sai Baba's temple for winning in sports.

2. D.I.A (Defence Intelligence Agency) - For "DIA," we can imagine a "Diya" (lamp). Visualize defence personnel holding a lamp, representing the Defence Intelligence Agency.

3. P.O.T.A (Prevention of Terrorism Act) - For "POTA," imagine a "pot" (container). Picture terrorists holding pots instead of weapons.

We can use imaginative pictures to remember abbreviations effectively. For example:

W.C.A.R (World Confrence Against Racism) - "W" can be visualized as "We" and "CAR" can be seen as an actual car. Imagine all of us sitting in a car heading to a conference to eliminate racism. This way, the words turn into images, and by connecting them, they are remembered as a visual scene.

This imaginative method turns abstract abbreviations into memorable visual stories, making them easier to recall.

❒

11

Name, Face, Personality Association

Have you ever noticed that when you ask someone their name and they tell you, you often don't remember their name after the conversation? You end up asking again, "What was your name?" Sometimes, you save a contact number with a name in your phone, but when you need it, you can't find it because you can't remember the name you saved it under. Often, we find ourselves saying, "What was the name of that person we met at the wedding?" and we can't recall it. This happens with the names of office officials, plumbers, electricians, bankers, teachers, and others we frequently deal with.

There are many people we frequently interact with, yet often we can't recall their names when needed. A hallmark of a good personality is remembering names. When you address someone by their name, it leaves a good impression. Let's understand why names are usually forgotten and how to remember them better.

Name, Face, Personality Association

When we first meet someone, it's normal to ask their name and, nowadays, to save their name and number in our mobile phones. Yet, we frequently forget the names. Why does this happen? Why do we sometimes fail to remember who we met?

Even with people we interact with regularly, their names might slip our minds at crucial moments. Remembering names is essential for making a positive impression. Addressing people by their names shows attentiveness and respect. Here's why names are often forgotten and how you can remember them effectively.

We often say, "Your face looks familiar, but I can't remember your name." You've probably never heard anyone say, "I remember your name, but I can't recall your face." Saying that would sound quite funny. The point here is that our brain remembers faces but often forgets names. The reason is that we see faces and hear names. Generally, we retain two types of memory: visual (seen) and auditory (heard). The strongest type of memory is visual, while auditory memory is relatively weaker. A face is a visual memory, and a name is an auditory memory. If we can associate an auditory memory with a visual image and connect it to a person's face or some characteristic, it greatly enhances the likelihood of remembering the name. Before delving into how to do this, let's discuss some common mistakes. When someone tells us their name, we often hear it as a formality, meaning we hear it with our ears but don't pay attention. Consequently, we keep asking for their name repeatedly. From now on, when you ask someone their name or they tell you, repeat it back immediately. For example, if someone says, "My name is Rajneesh," respond with, "Hello, Rajneesh." Use their name six or seven times during the conversation, and conclude by addressing them by name: "Rajneesh, what's your phone number?" This practice signals to your brain that the name is important, and it will retain it better.

Another method is associating the name with a face and personality. Create an image for the name and link it to a distinctive feature of the person's face, profession, or personality. For instance, if someone's name is Rajkumar and they have a big beard, imagine film actor Rajkumar holding this person's beard. The next time you see this person, noticing their beard will remind you of the funny image of Rajkumar holding it, helping you recall that the person's name is Rajkumar. It might sound strange, but it's effective. Try it out and see for yourself.

❐

12

Logical Memory

If we classify studying, it mainly falls into two categories: logic (logical principles) and facts. Logic involves content based on principles that need to be understood first, while facts require direct memorization. In logic, understanding is crucial, whereas in facts, memorization is key. The primary difference between logic and facts is that logical content allows the brain to create a platform memory.

Platform memory refers to a designated place in the brain for storing information, much like how we have logical places for items in our homes. For example, clothes go in the closet, food in the refrigerator, books on the bookshelf, and utensils in the kitchen. These are logical platforms for storing these items, so we look for them in these respective places. Similarly, when studying logical content, the brain creates a platform memory and connects new information to this existing memory.

For instance, in mathematics, you need to fully understand the content. Mathematics is a subject that requires comprehension. Once you grasp a basic principle, you can solve subsequent problems based on that principle. The same applies to science, where most of the content is logical. For example, understanding why objects fall involves grasping the concept of gravity. Once you understand this rule, it applies to everything.

Understanding logical memory is crucial for effective studying. Study materials can be divided into two main categories:

logical principles (logic) and factual information (facts). Logical content involves principles that must be understood, while facts require straightforward memorization.

Logical subjects rely on understanding. Once a foundational principle is understood, it can be applied to solve various problems. For example, in mathematics, understanding that two plus two equals four helps in understanding that two plus three equals five. You don't need to memorize each individual sum because you understand the logic of addition.

In contrast, facts do not rely on logic. For instance, knowing that the capital of India is New Delhi does not help in determining the capital of Australia, which also needs to be memorized. Another difference between logic and facts is the time required to understand and memorize them. Logical content takes longer to understand initially, but once understood, it takes less time to remember. On the other hand, factual content takes less time to understand but more time to memorize.

To differentiate between logical and factual content, consider the nature of the questions involved. Questions that ask "who," "where," "when," and "what" are factual, while questions that ask "why" and "how" are logical. The advantage of logic is that once you understand the main argument, you can derive answers to similar questions using the same logic.

For example, in mathematics, once you understand the logic that two plus two equals four, you can easily understand how to add other numbers without having to memorize each sum individually. In contrast, factual information such as the capitals of countries must be memorized individually because there is no underlying logic connecting them.

In summary, logical memory helps in understanding and retaining concepts, reducing the need for repetitive study. Once you grasp the fundamental logic, it becomes easier to apply it to various problems, making studying more efficient.

Logical Memory

In logical memory, once you fully understand a particular example, it becomes a foundation on which you can solve other examples based on the same principle. Let's understand this with an example.

If asked, "What is 25 multiplied by 25?" the answer would be 625. How do we know this? Because we learned how to multiply in our childhood. You write 25 under 25, multiply 5 by 5, then 5 by 2, then multiply 2 by 5 and 2 by 2. After adding these results, you get 625.

This process illustrates how understanding the basic principle of multiplication allows you to apply it to different numbers without needing to memorize each multiplication result individually. The logic of multiplication is the underlying principle that helps you solve any multiplication problem by applying the same steps.

This is the traditional method. But can you find the answer to 35 multiplied by 35 or 45 multiplied by 45 based on this principle, using a method different from traditional ones? Today, I will teach you a technique that will not only help you quickly solve such questions but also enable you to use the same memory to quickly multiply other similar questions. This technique can also be applied to other numbers ending in 5, such as 35 or 45. Let's try it:

For 35 × 35:

1. Separate the numbers into 3 and 5.
2. Multiply 5 by 5 to get 25.
3. Add 1 to one of the 3s to get 4, so you now have 3 and 4.

4. Multiply 3 by 4 to get 12.
5. Write 25 next to 12, making it 1225.

For 45 × 45:

1. Separate the numbers into 4 and 5.
2. Multiply 5 by 5 to get 25.
3. Add 1 to one of the 4s to get 5, so you now have 4 and 5.
4. Multiply 4 by 5 to get 20.
5. Write 25 next to 20, making it 2025.

This method leverages a logical pattern and visual memory to make the multiplication process quicker and more intuitive.

Isn't that a different logical method? Based on the same principle, let's multiply 35 by 35. Separate 3 and 3 to one side and 5 and 5 to the other side. Now, multiply 5 by 5 to get 25 and set it aside. You are left with 3 and 3. Add 1 to one of the 3s to get 4, which makes it 4 and 3. Now, multiply these two to get 12. Write 12 before 25, making it 1225. This is the answer. Similarly, you can find the squares of all such numbers that end in 5 using this method. The key learning point is that once you understand the logical basis, you can solve similar types of questions easily.

Look at the number 25 in your mind and write 25 below it. Now separate the 2 and 2, and the 5 and 5. Multiply 5 by 5 and set it aside, which will always be 25. Now take the 2 and 2 left, add one to one of the numbers, making it 3. So now you have 3 and 2. Multiply these two numbers to get 6. Now write 25 next to 6, making it 625. Isn't that different?

This method leverages a logical pattern and visual memory to make the multiplication process quicker and more intuitive.

Isn't that a different logical method? Based on the same principle, let's multiply 35 by 35. Separate 3 and 3 to one side and 5 and 5 to the other side. Now, multiply 5 by 5 to get 25 and set it aside. You are left with 3 and 3. Add 1 to one of the 3s to get 4, which makes it 4 and 3. Now, multiply these two to get 12. Write 12 before 25, making it 1225. This is the answer.

Similarly, you can find the squares of all such numbers that end in 5 using this method. The key learning point is that once you understand the logical basis, you can solve similar types of questions easily.

❐

(13)

Memorization - The Fourth Dimension of Education

The vehicle of education runs on four wheels: reading, writing, understanding, and memorizing. We often excel at reading, writing, and understanding, but we struggle with memorizing effectively. Consequently, we never forget how to read, write, and understand, but we often forget what we've memorized. This is why we need to keep repeating information to retain it, making memorization the most time-consuming part of studying. The traditional method of repetition or rote learning is outdated. Fundamentally, the brain registers information in four ways, converting it into memory. This process is called memorization.

Memorization

The brain registers information and converts it into memory in four ways:

1. *Emotional Connection*: Information that we have an emotional connection with it. So, our brain retains information with an emotional connection. For example, we might not remember everyone's phone numbers, but we do remember the numbers of our close friends, life partners, or parents because of our emotional connection with them. This emotional bond leads our brain to memorize these details, and we rarely forget them.

2. *Logical Information*: The brain retains information that is logical, has reasoning, or is based on principles. Once we understand these logically, they stay with us without needing frequent repetition. For instance, mathematics requires logical understanding. Once we grasp it fully, we don't need to keep revising it. Addition and subtraction, which we learned in the early grades, stay with us forever, even though we don't practice them regularly anymore.

3. *Repetition*: This is the most traditional method. It involves repeating information multiple times to remember it, and the brain registers it through frequency, creating memory. However, it is also the weakest method because even if information is memorized through repetition, the brain may forget it after some time, necessitating constant review for it to stay remembered.

Repetition takes the most time to remember, and once you stop repeating, you start forgetting. That's why we don't retain the entire curriculum from our early school years, even if we scored well.

4. *Visual Information*: This type of information is powerful and forms our most dominant memory. The brain remembers best by seeing and retains it for the longest time. For example, we often remember movies because we watch them. Even after watching a movie once, we can recall its story and scenes. By using these four methods, the brain turns information into memory. The coordination of these methods is used in mnemonics.

❒

(14)

Life Principle

The most important task of our brain is to store information correctly and retrieve it when needed, which we call recollection. Receiving information is known as memorization, storing it in the brain is called retention, and recalling it is known as recollection. While we memorize everything, not everything comes to mind easily because recollection depends on where and how the information is stored in the brain. To store information properly, we need association. Today, we will learn what to do for good retention.

Life Principle: L.I.F.E. Principle

To store any information, the brain needs a platform. A platform means a place to store things. At home, things get lost if they don't have a designated place. Things that have a platform or a place to keep them don't get lost.

To create a good and strong platform, we can use the L.I.F.E. principle. The first letter of LIFE is 'L' - which stands for 'Link'. Linking information together serves as a strong platform for storing information.

For example, to prevent keys from getting lost, we link them with a key-chain and hang them on a large hook on the wall to find them easily. This is a very good example of linking. Similarly, information should be linked together in the brain to remember it.

'I' stands for Imagination - Seeing information in your imagination helps to remember it very well and creates a solid platform. Imagining something once is equivalent to repeating it twenty times. Whatever you are reading or trying to remember, you should imagine it in your mind. This is effective for good memory retention.

'F' stands for Faith - Before doing any task, having faith in yourself and your brain is very important. If we remember with full confidence and believe that remembering is easy for the brain and that we will never forget, the brain creates a platform and retains it.

'E' stands for Emotions - Information has a greater impact on the brain when it brings about emotional changes. When watching a movie, the story and characters get linked with our emotions, which makes it easier to remember.We cannot forget the things that our brain creates a strong platform for, even if we want to. Therefore, while trying to remember anything, if we emotionally feel the information, a platform will be created in the brain, and it will always be remembered.

❐

(15)

Question Letter Method

The human brain is like a house. Just as a house has rooms where things are kept, each item is placed in a specific location and categorized accordingly. For example, utensils are kept in the kitchen, clothes in the wardrobe, sleeping arrangements in the bedroom, meals are eaten in the dining room, and there is a drawing room for guests.

There will be a storeroom for unnecessary items, etc. Similarly, the brain also works this way. The brain is like a house of information and uses logic to store this information. Information placed in its appropriate spot according to logic is never lost. However, information stored haphazardly in the brain without using logic often gets misplaced and does not come to mind, which we perceive as forgetting. In reality, we don't forget anything; we just misplace the information.

Question Letter Method

Often, we make mistakes in remembering the order of sequential answers. The information is in our minds but gets confused. Even after memorizing, chronological answers often confuse us. Let's learn a method to remember such questions, called the Question Letter Method. As the name suggests, we can use the letters of the question to help remember the answer.

As I mentioned earlier, if we create a logical place for things in the brain-like house, they will be established in the designated spot. In this method, we will use the letters of the question's root word as a logical platform. For example, the chronological list of Gupta dynasty kings is as follows: the first king is Sri Gupta, followed by Chandragupta, Samudragupta, Chandragupta Vikramaditya, Kumaragupta, and Skandagupta. Now, to remember this in chronological order, and that too permanently, For this, look at the letters of the root word. The root word spelling is G U P T A. We will use these letters you can give an imaginary meaning to the letters of the question's root word and link it to the answer.

For instance, the first letter is 'G,' and 'G' stands for 'Girl' as an imaginary meaning. 'U' stands for 'Umbrella,' 'P' for 'Parrot,' 'T' for 'Tiger,' and 'A' for 'Apple.' Now, let's remember the order of the Gupta dynasty. The common element here is 'Gupta,' so there's no need to remember it. We only need to remember the main names of the kings. The first king is Sri Gupta; logically, we consider that he was the founding king, hence the indicative 'Sri' in his name. So, the name is Sri Gupta. The next is Chandragupta; imagine a 'G' - Girl sitting on the moon (Chandra). The next king is Samudragupta; think of a large 'U' - Umbrella in the middle of the ocean (Samudra). Then comes Chandragupta Vikramaditya; imagine that instead of Betal on the king's back, there is a 'P' - Parrot. The next king is Kumaragupta; visualize a potter making large 'T' - Tigers out of clay.

The last one is Skandagupta. Let's associate 'Skand' (which means shoulder) with the letter 'A' - for Apple. Imagine having an apple on each of your shoulders. Now, let's think about the order of the Gupta dynasty kings. To recall this, just focus on the letters of the question. We remembered the first king logically as Sri Gupta, as he was the founding king.

Next, think of 'G' - Girl. Where was the girl sitting? On the moon, so it's Chandragupta. After that? 'U' - for Umbrella, which will remind you of Samudragupta. Isn't this logic amazing?

❐

(16)

Sleep Management and Revision Plan

During exams, there's pressure to score good marks and cover the syllabus. You might have heard that during exam days, students often reduce their sleep time to increase their study time.

Sleep Management and Revision Plan

During exam periods, there's pressure to score well and cover the syllabus. You might have heard that students often reduce their sleeping hours to increase study time during exams. They stay up all night, continuously revising and memorizing, but despite studying all night, they often make mistakes in exams. Do you know how staying up late affects your brain? Is staying up all night really necessary for good results? Stress is high during exams, and many students develop a habit of staying awake to study, which disrupts their sleep cycle. Remember, while you sleep, your brain doesn't actually rest; instead, it reorganizes the information collected throughout the day. In other words, your sleep time is also the time when your brain reorganizes and stores information. The brain needs a full eight hours of sleep to effectively process and organize this information. Have you ever felt more tired after waking up late on a holiday compared to your usual wake-up time of 6 AM? If you take a nap during the day, do you also feel groggy upon waking? This happens because you're disrupting your body's regular sleep cycle. Students who stay up all night studying during exams often make mistakes because their sleep cycle is disrupted. When the sleep cycle is broken, the brain doesn't get enough time to consolidate information, which means many details aren't firmly stored and may not be recalled during the exam.

Just as exercise is essential for building and maintaining physical strength, eight hours of sleep is crucial for keeping the brain healthy and effective. An hour of study before bed can be beneficial, but only for revision, not for new or unclear material. Since revision allows you to cover more material in less time and the content is already understood, this time is very suitable for it.

You will get good marks not by staying up all night, but by getting proper sleep at night.

❒

(17)

Specific Meaning Association

Self-Meaning Association

It is well known that good general knowledge turns a person into a remarkable individual. Everyone wants to remember and retain general knowledge, but often finds it difficult because it is highly factual. Today, we will learn how to remember these facts. We will use the principles of association and imagination to achieve this.

***Jalandhar - Sports Goods*:** Imagine your sports equipment floating inside water (Jal), symbolizing Jalandhar.

***Katni - Cement*:** Picture a cut on your knee (Nee) being treated not with medicine but with cement.

***Jharia - Coal*:** Visualize bushes filled with coal.

***Kerala - Coffee*:** Imagine dipping a bitter gourd (Karela) into coffee and eating it.

***Rubber - Karnataka*:** Picture your friend giving you rubber toys and asking you to perform a play (naty) on stage, representing Karnataka.

***Rice - West Bengal*:** Envision a large mansion (Bangla) filled with rice, symbolizing West Bengal.

Now, all you need to do is visualize these imaginary images linked to the names. This will help you recall the answers easily. For instance, if I ask where coffee is produced, you'll immediately remember the image of dipping bitter gourd in coffee, and the answer "Kerala" will come to mind. Isn't it easy and interesting?

❒

18

The ABCDE of the Mind

(A. B. C. D. E)

Everyone desires to score good marks in their studies. Nowadays, people are studying day and night to achieve this. There are four pillars of good academic performance: reading, writing, understanding, and memorizing. Among these, memorizing is the most crucial because exams test your memory. No matter how much you have read, written, or understood, if you cannot recall it during the exam, you won't score well.

And to ensure that you remember well and on time, it's important to memorize effectively. The better you memorize, the quicker you'll recall the information. Today, let's learn how to perceive information in a way that makes it stick in your memory.

ABCDE Principle

The brain stores information in two ways: either as ordinary information or as specific information. Information preserved visually in the mind is recalled quickly. To make any information solid and specific, you should understand this principle and apply it to your studies.

***A - Action*:** Information that is associated with an action is remembered more effectively by our brain. For example, movies are automatically remembered because all the information and scenes in them are action-oriented.

***B - Big*:** Information that is large in size or has a big impact is better remembered by the brain. Think about what comes to mind first when you recall a fair you attended—it's usually the big swings and rides.

***C - Colorful*:** Things that are colorful attract more attention. For example, in newspapers or books, your attention is drawn more to colorful information than to black-and-white text.

***D - Dimensional*:** Things perceived in a three-dimensional form are remembered more easily. For instance, when you hear the word "airplane," an image of an airplane immediately comes to mind. But if the word is "confidence," no specific image appears instantly.

***E - Emotional*:** Information that has an emotional impact on the brain is remembered more quickly. For example, if you need to recall who ranked first in this year's Civil Services (IAS) exam, you might struggle to remember. But if that person is your brother, son, or friend, you won't forget because of the emotional connection.

If you apply this principle while studying, by perceiving every piece of information or subject matter in this way, it will be easier to remember and will come to mind quickly during exams.

❐

(19)

Imaginary Logic Method

Today's topic is especially relevant for commerce students and taxpayers, but it will be useful for everyone. Friends, there are times when we need to remember information that is entirely factual, and due to the lack of specific logic, we have to repeat it over and over again. Sometimes, the subject matter can be very confusing because it looks very similar to other information, like the sections and subsections of income tax for commerce students.

Let's learn how to remember such things effectively.

Imaginary Logic Method

In this method, we focus on the part of the information that needs to be remembered and create an imaginary logic that connects it to the key point of the answer. For example, consider the sections of income tax—like *Section 80C*—which provides tax exemptions on insurance, savings, and long-term investments.

To remember this, you can imagine an 80-year-old Cow (representing "80C") calmly grazing, which symbolizes stability and long-term benefits, thus linking it to insurance, savings, and investments that offer tax benefits over time.

***Section 80D*:** Tax exemption on health insurance premiums.

***Section 80DD*:** Tax relief on expenses for the treatment of a dependent with a disability.

***Section 80U*:** Tax relief on treatment expenses if you yourself have a disability.

***Section 80E*:** Tax relief on interest paid for an education loan.

***Section 80G*:** Tax relief on donations made.

***Section 80GG*:** Tax relief on house rent.

Remembering such subject matter can be difficult because "Section 80" is common in all of them, leading to confusion. Let's focus on remembering the key points by associating them with the letters that follow "80."

For example:

80C: Connect "C" with "Collection"—imagine how you collect savings for emergencies or future needs, linking it to tax exemptions on insurance, savings, and long-term investments.

Now, let's create similar associations for the others:

80D: Link "D" to "Doctor"—think of a doctor prescribing health insurance, which is tax-exempt.

80DD: Associate "DD" with "Dependent Disability"—imagine caring for a dependent with a disability, and getting tax relief for it.

80U: "U" could stand for "U" (yourself)—picture yourself dealing with a disability, and getting tax exemption on treatment costs.

80E: Connect "E" with "Education"—visualize a student taking out an education loan and receiving tax relief on the interest.

80G: Link "G" with "Giving"—imagine donating to a charity and getting tax relief.

80GG: Connect "GG" with "Guesthouse" or "Ghar" (home)—picture yourself paying rent for a house and receiving a tax exemption.

By focusing on these key letters and their associations, you can reduce confusion and recall the information more easily.

❐

(20)

Rhyming Method and Mental Clock

Harmony Method: Mind Clock

You may have noticed that the most important things are often the ones we tend to forget. With so many tasks in a day, we often remember the essential ones only when we return home. This happens especially when there are multiple tasks to manage in a single day. This is because the brain focuses only on highly significant and serious thoughts. However, if the tasks are linked with some creative mnemonic, you will remember them all.

Harmony Rhyming Method - Mind Clock System

Often, we forget appointments or tasks scheduled for a specific time. The entire day passes, and we only remember when the work is already done or the time has passed, like when you realize you missed a doctor's appointment. Let's learn how to use the "Mind Clock" system to remember these tasks so that nothing slips through the cracks! As the name of this method suggests, the Rhyming Method involves linking a specific time with a rhyming word that helps you remember it. You can create your own rhyme or use the suggested ones below. In the clock, numbers can be replaced by these rhyming words:

- 1 o'clock - Sun
- 2 o'clock - Shoe

- 3 o'clock - Tree
- 4 o'clock - Door
- 5 o'clock - Knife (chalk)
- 6 o'clock - Bees
- 7 o'clock - Heaven
- 8 o'clock - Plate
- 9 o'clock - Wine
- 10 o'clock - Hen
- 11 o'clock - Lemon (knee)
- 12 o'clock - Shell (Torch or Light)

Now, let's say I have to go to the gym at 7 AM, then to the railway station at 9 AM, deposit money at the bank at 10 AM, pick up the kids from school at 1 PM, have lunch at a friend's house at 2 PM, meet the doctor at 3 PM, and go swimming at the pool at 4 PM. To remember all these tasks, you can link them as follows:

- ***7 AM (Heaven)*:** Imagine you are working out in heaven.
- ***9 AM (Wine)*:** Picture a train at the railway station loaded with wine.
- ***10 AM (Hen)*:** Visualize a hen depositing money at the bank.
- ***1 PM (Sun)*:** Imagine that the kids' school is on the sun.
- ***2 PM (Shoe)*:** Picture having lunch with a friend, and someone has placed a shoe on the dining table.
- ***3 PM (Tree)*:** Imagine the doctor is sitting on a tree, treating patients.
- ***4 PM (Door)*:** Visualize that as soon as you open the door, there's a swimming pool outside. Now, whenever

you look at the clock and try to remember what task you need to do at a particular time, the rhyming images will remind you of your tasks. For example, if I ask, "When is the doctor's appointment?" you will recall that the doctor was sitting on a tree, and "tree" rhymes with 3, so the appointment is at 3 PM. Similarly, if you need to remember what task is at 4 PM, you will remember that behind the "door" (4), there's a swimming pool, so you need to go swimming.

Isn't the Mind Clock System effective?

❐

21

Absent-Mindedness and Latent Learning

Once, my nephew Chintu was having dinner at the dining table. His mother came and said, "Chintu, I forgot to bring salt from the kitchen. Go and get the salt." Chintu replied, "Mom, I won't be able to find the salt. You should get it yourself." His mother insisted, "You always do this! You have to get it. Go to the kitchen; it's on the fridge, in the red bottle. Hurry up and get it!" Chintu still hesitated, saying, "Mom, I won't find it, you get it." His mother warned, "If you don't go now, you'll be in trouble. Go and get it!" Reluctantly, Chintu went to the kitchen, but soon called out, "I can't find the salt anywhere!" His mother replied, "Look properly! It's right there on the fridge. Don't make me come there." Chintu insisted, "I'm telling you, I really can't see it." Frustrated, his mother walked into the kitchen, grabbed Chintu by the ear, and scolded him, "Look! It's right here in front of you! And you couldn't see it? You always make excuses when asked to do something!" Chintu protested, "No, Mom, I honestly didn't see it!"

Has something similar ever happened to you? Even when something is right in front of us, sometimes we just can't seem to find it until someone else points it out. Do you know why this happens?

Absent-Mindedness and Latent Learning

Scientists explain that when we are given a task, our mind often creates an imaginary outcome for that task. This imaginary outcome usually aligns with the actual result. This process of mentally picturing the outcome before it happens is called latent learning. Sometimes, this imagined result can influence the real outcome. Whether you like the task or not, your brain automatically creates an imaginary outcome for it.

For example, when Chintu was told to bring the salt, his immediate response was, "I won't be able to find it." This statement was interpreted by his brain as the desired outcome, creating a mental process where Chintu could see everything except the salt, leading to him not finding it. This is known as absent-mindedness. Chintu's negative statement, "I won't find the salt," caused his brain to equate success with not finding the salt.

Remember, your brain always wants you to succeed. But success depends on your thoughts and your initial approach to the task. When you approach a task with positive thoughts, your brain becomes more attentive, leading to positive imagined outcomes and, ultimately, positive real results, helping you succeed. From now on, whenever you take on a task, always start with a positive statement to yourself, and watch how your brain helps you achieve success.

❒

22

Mental Linking System

Friends, a sharp mind makes every challenge easier—this is an eternal truth. Often, we forget where we've placed things at home. Sometimes, we can't find our keys, socks, or handkerchiefs; other times, we lose our mobile phones and have to call them from another phone to locate them. Sometimes, a pen goes missing, and other times, we can't find the electricity bill. We might forget where we've kept important documents. Today, let's learn how to remember where we've placed things at home so that we can find them when needed.

Mental Linking System

Items in the house get lost when they don't have a designated place, but things that have a fixed spot never get lost. You might often hear someone say they can't find their pen, checkbook, or Aadhar card, but you'll rarely hear someone say they can't find the tomatoes—because tomatoes have a designated spot in the fridge. We've formed an association between the fridge and the items kept in it, which helps us remember that food and drinks are stored in the fridge. Other items, however, are placed randomly without any association, which is why we often forget where we've kept them. Let's learn how to ensure we remember all the things we want to keep track of.

Our minds remember large, active items and scenes more effectively, so by creating imaginary scenes, we can firmly remember where things are kept at home. For instance, if you tend to forget where you placed your keys, you can stick a label on them that says "elephant" and imagine that you're placing a large elephant somewhere in your house instead of the keys. This way, you'll always remember where the keys are because as soon as you think of the keys, you'll picture the elephant and remember where it's "standing" in the house.

When placing a pen, imagine that it's the world's largest pen, which is enormous in size, and you'll always remember where you kept it. When storing your Aadhaar card or important documents, picture the Aadhaar card as being gigantic and on fire, with the documents constantly burning. You'll remember where this imaginary fire is in the house. If you have trouble finding your checkbook when you need it, imagine, when you first store it, that it is gradually growing larger and is filled with millions of rupees. By using these simple yet powerful associative techniques, you can ensure that you never forget where you've placed anything at home.

❐

23

The Shape Method

Information in our brain is primarily stored in five forms: taste, smell, touch, sound, and visuals. Among these, visual information is the most powerful and enduring. It represents the most natural and potent form of human memory. If we convert any information into a visual form, it can be transformed into long-term memory.

The Shape Method

We've been learning and seeing numbers in a certain form since childhood, but these forms are often abstract, making numerical information difficult to remember. However, if we assign each number a new three-dimensional visual form, those numbers can help us build lasting memories. You can create a form for each number based on its shape. For example:

- The number 1 resembles a stick.
- The number 2 resembles a duck.
- The number 3 has the shape of a heart.
- The number 4 looks like a flag.
- The number 5 resembles a hook.
- The number 6 has the shape of a hockey stick.
- The number 7 looks like a lamp post.
- The number 8 resembles a pair of glasses.

- The number 9 resembles a lollipop.
- The number 10 can be visualized as a bat and ball.

Now, let's say you want to remember the Presidents of India in order. You can create a visual representation for each President and associate it with these numbers:

1. **The first President, *Rajendra Prasad*** – imagine a king (a visual representation of "Raja") holding a stick (representing the number 1).
2. **The second President, *Sarvepalli Radhakrishnan*** – visualize Radha and Lord Krishna, and imagine a duck worshiping them (representing the number 2).
3. **The third President, *Zakir Husain*** – imagine Zakir Husain (the tabla player) playing a tabla shaped like a heart (representing the number 3).
4. **The fourth President, *V. V. Giri*** – picture Giri's wife holding the national flag (representing the number 4).

By creating such visual representations, you can not only remember the Presidents but also any sequence you need to recall. This method allows you to create vivid, imaginative images that are linked to the information you want to remember, making it much easier to retain in your memory.

❐

(24)

Number Picture System

Friends, do you know that our mind uses imagination to remember things and association to recall them? Our brain quickly remembers things when it can create a three-dimensional image of them. For example, if I say "white horse," your mind immediately conjures an image of a white horse. But if I say "priority," your mind might struggle to create a clear picture because it's an abstract concept. These are what we call abstract words. The brain easily forms associations with concrete words and helps recall them faster.

Number Picture System

Numbers are also abstract concepts, which is why it's relatively harder to remember numbers or things related to them. Whether it's phone numbers, important dates, or numbers related to your studies like atomic numbers, melting points, square roots, etc. In this method, we can transform numbers into concrete images and use them to remember a specific sequence. For example:

- The number 1 can be represented by a king, as there is only one king.
- The number 2 can be represented by eyes, as we have two eyes.
- The number 3 can be represented by monkeys, as Gandhi Ji's three monkeys are famous.

- The number 4 can be visualized as a car, since a car has four wheels.
- The number 5 can be represented by the five fingers of a hand.
- The number 6 can be visualized as cricket, as it relates to a "six" in the game.
- The number 7 can be depicted as a rainbow because it has seven colors.
- The number 8 can be an octopus with eight arms.
- The number 9 can be represented by the nine planets of our solar system.
- The number 10 can be visualized as Ravana, who had ten heads.

Now, whatever sequence you want to remember, you can easily associate it with these new symbols for numbers. How? Let's use these to remember the five layers of the atmosphere. The five layers are:

1. Troposphere
2. Stratosphere
3. Mesosphere
4. Thermosphere
5. Exosphere

You don't need to remember "sphere" since it's common in all layers. You just need to remember the main names, which are abstract words. So let's give them imaginary concrete forms:

- The first layer is "Troposphere," which can be associated with a "topi" (hat) because it sounds similar. Imagine a king (number 1) wearing a hat.

- The second layer is "Stratosphere," which can be associated with a "straw." Imagine you are lifting a straw with your two eyes (number 2).
- The third layer is "Mesosphere," which can be associated with "moje" (socks). Picture monkeys (number 3) wearing your socks.
- The fourth layer is "Thermosphere," which can be associated with a "thermometer." Imagine thermometers placed in a car (number 4).
- The fifth layer is "Exosphere," which can be associated with an "axe." Imagine holding a large axe with your five fingers (number 5).

Now, if someone asks you, "What is the name of the third layer of the atmosphere?" First, you recall the image for number 3, which is monkeys. Then you remember that the monkeys were wearing socks, leading you to recall that the third layer is the "Mesosphere."

Isn't it easy to remember sequences using numbers?

❒

25

Visual Linking Method

Sometimes, we need to remember information that is interconnected. However, despite our efforts, we might not recall all parts of that information. This often happens because we rely on repetition or rote memorization, which doesn't create lasting memories. Repeatedly memorized information isn't stable, and it depends heavily on continuous repetition. But if you visualize the information in your mind while repeating it, it becomes more stable. This is because one piece of information reinforces the other.

Visual Linking Method

In this method, two pieces of information are linked together to aid memory. The key requirement is that both pieces of information should be visualized in a concrete form.

Using this method, we can remember many important associations, such as inventions and their inventors, places and their products, mineral sources and their locations, terminology, etc. For instance:

- The inventor of the telephone is *Graham Bell*.
- The inventor of the elevator is *Otis*.
- The inventor of the revolver is *Colt*.
- The inventor of the typewriter is *Sholes*.
- The inventor of the steamboat is **Fulton**.

To remember these, notice that there are two pieces of information: one is the invention, and the other is the inventor. The special thing here is that the invention already has a concrete image in our minds. For example, when we think of a typewriter, an image of it immediately comes to mind. However, the inventor's name doesn't have a concrete form in our mind, so this is what we need to remember.

Here's what you need to do: First, take the abstract information (the inventor's name) and give it an imaginary, concrete form. Then, associate this with the already concrete form of the invention.

For example:

- ***Telephone - Graham Bell*:** Imagine the bell of a telephone becoming extremely hot (a play on "Graham" as "Hot Bell").
- ***Elevator - Otis*:** Picture an elevator in an office (Otis sounds like "Office").
- ***Revolver - Colt*:** Imagine hiding a revolver in the pocket of a coat (Colt sounds like "Coat").
- ***Typewriter - Sholes*:** Visualize a typewriter wrapped in a shawl (Sholes sounds like "Shawl").
- ***Steamboat - Fulton*:** Imagine a steamboat filled with a ton of flowers (Fulton sounds like "Full-ton").

By using this method, you can easily remember various types of associations.

❐

(26)

Emotional Experience Method

What's the best way to do something well? It's to learn it thoroughly. Our brain stores memories in various forms, but the most significant one is **experiential memory**. When we experience an event that triggers an emotional response, that event becomes a permanent memory in our brain. Information that has a direct emotional connection with us is more likely to be retained as a lasting memory.

Emotional Experience Method

In this method, an event is imagined in such a way that it evokes an emotional response, making the information or event permanently memorable. For instance, reading about an accident might not leave a lasting memory. Hearing about it might help you remember it somewhat better. But witnessing an accident will likely make the memory stick for a long time. However, if you actually experience the accident, it becomes an unforgettable, permanent memory. There are many things we don't want to remember, but we still do because the event caused a strong emotional impact on our brain at the time.

This means that all these memories are tied to emotional experiences. We can use this same process positively to remember things we want to keep in mind.

For example, if you want to remember details about *Tipu Sultan*, you could imagine that Tipu Sultan is a member of your own family or even that you are Tipu Sultan yourself. Then, as you study the events related to him, you'll be able to experience these events through your imagination, making them easier to remember.

Let's say you need to remember the **Mysore War** between Tipu Sultan and the British. To make this memory stick, you could imagine that Tipu Sultan and the British are fighting right in your neighborhood over who gets to go to Mysore. You picture yourself trying to mediate the fight, telling them to stop. This imagination helps you remember the event better because it's tied to your emotions.

Similarly, if you need to remember that Raniganj is famous for coal production**, you could imagine a queen (Rani) who has become bald (ganj) because she carried burning coals on her head. This queen is your friend, and you are taking her to the hospital. You'll find that this memory sticks easily because you've created an emotional connection with the information. Interesting, isn't it? You can try this technique yourself and see how well it works!

❐

(27)

The Cinematic Visualization Method

Today, we'll explore a unique process that our brain uses for memory preservation. To firmly establish information in the brain, it often gives that information a form or structure. Just like a computer that stores data in binary code—0s and 1s—even though we retrieve the data as pictures, videos, text, or numbers, it's all stored in binary. Similarly, the brain stores information by giving it a form. It primarily stores facts in three forms: words, images, and movies. If we want to convert a fact into a permanent memory, we can transform these three forms into a mental movie using our imagination.

Cinematic Visualization Method

In this method, you visualize a sequence of facts as a series of mental movies. For instance, let's take an example from geography: the factors affecting the environment—

1. Forest Area,
2. Soil Types,
3. Industrial Areas,
4. Distance from the Sea,
5. Mountainous Areas,
6. Clouds.

To remember these facts in order, you can create a mental movie by linking one fact to another sequentially. Imagine you are searching for a good environment, so you enter a forest where you find various types of soil. You pick up some soil and place it in a large industrial factory. This factory is floating on the sea. By the sea, there's a large mountain, and as you climb it, you see thick clouds covering the mountain top.

Now, you'll find it much easier to remember these factors because our brains retain visual sequences more effectively than plain text. Try recalling the sequence without rereading the list—you'll see how effortlessly you remember it through this mental movie!

❐

(28)

The Mnemonic Abbreviation Method

Hello friends! Our brain always tries to connect new memories with existing ones to make them permanent. This means that if we link something unforgettable to something we want to remember, we can turn new information into a permanent memory. One effective way to do this is by creating a mnemonic abbreviation.

*Mnemonic Abbreviation Method**

This method helps you remember essential factual information that follows a specific sequence. In this technique, to remember any sequence—whether it is in ascending, descending, or any other order—you create a new sentence by combining the first letters of each word from the facts. By memorizing this sentence, you can easily recall the points and the sequence of facts.

For example, consider the sentence, "Chhat Par Ja Gabar Maami Hai, Unhe Cancer Hai." This sentence helps you remember the states in India that lie on the Tropic of Cancer: **Ch**hattisgarh, **T**ripura, Jharkhand, *Gujarat, *Bengal, Rajasthan, Madhya Pradesh, and *Mizoram. The first letters of each state are combined to form this quirky sentence, making it easier to remember.

Another example is remembering the neighboring countries of India that share both land and sea borders: Myanmar, Bangladesh, and Pakistan. You can create the mnemonic "Maa

Baap" where "Maa" stands for Myanmar, "Ba" for Bangladesh, and "P" for Pakistan. Imagine that all parents ("Maa-Baap") prefer to travel to countries connected to India by both land and sea—this visualization reinforces the memory.

Similarly, the sentence "Kek Gaya Gum" helps you recall the states located on India's western coast: Kerala, Karnataka, *Goa*, *Gujarat*, and *Maharashtra. By creating your own mnemonic sentences, you can easily memorize difficult sequences or pieces of information.

This method simplifies the memorization process and makes it more fun, allowing you to recall complex information effortlessly!

❐

29

Vocabulary Memorization Technique

Friends, in this chapter, we will learn how to remember English words, their meanings, and even the entire dictionary. A language has two main components: grammar and vocabulary. We don't forget grammar because it is based on logic and reasoning, but vocabulary is often forgotten even after repeated attempts because it is not based on principles or logic. Many people want to have a strong vocabulary. Let's learn how we can remember vocabulary, even an entire dictionary.

Dictionary Memorization Technique**

In this method, we use imagination to give each word a tangible form and link that imaginary form to its meaning. How? Let's look at an example:

Consider some English words and their meanings:

- ***Besmirch*:** This means to make dirty or tarnish. Imagine a scene where children scatter twenty chilies in your house, making it dirty. The word "besmirch" sounds like "twenty chilies" in Hindi, which helps you remember the meaning.
- ***Loiter*:** This means to wander aimlessly. Think of a "lighter" in the hands of people wandering around without purpose. The word "loiter" sounds like "lighter," which helps you recall the meaning.

- ***Bedizen*:** This means to decorate with ornaments. Imagine a big “Zen car” covered in decorations. The word “bedizen” can be associated with this image of a decorated Zen car.
- ***Arrack*:** This means old liquor. Picture an “arrack” (a shelf or rack) filled with old liquor. The word “arrack” sounds like “rack,” helping you remember the meaning.
- ***Murky*:** This means gloomy. Visualize a “murky” (a chicken) that looks very sad. The word “murky” can be associated with this sad chicken.
- ***Augment*:** This means to increase. Imagine adding mint to a fire, causing it to grow. The word “augment” can be connected to this image of a fire growing with mint.
- ***Gingerly*:** This means cautiously. Picture “ginger” with a caution sign. The word “gingerly” can be associated with this cautious ginger.
- ***Mutter*:** This means to mumble. Picture yourself with “mutter” (peas) in your mouth, making it hard to speak clearly, so you only mumble. The word “mutter” can be linked to this image.
- ***Lassitude*:** This means extreme fatigue. Imagine that you always drink “lassi” (a drink) when you are extremely tired. The word “lassitude” can be connected to this image of drinking lassi when exhausted.

Now, whenever you think of a word, visualize the tangible image in your mind. This image will help you recall the meaning of the word. For example, if I ask you the meaning of “murky,” recall the image of the sad chicken, and you’ll remember that “murky”means gloomy.

Isn’t it fun?

(30)

Doctor's Mindful Names

A few days ago, I had to visit the hospital. My friend's mother was undergoing treatment. We reached the ward, and I went to her bedside. Just then, a resident doctor came for rounds and checked on her. After reviewing the reports, he suggested, "You should show these reports to a gastroenterologist and get their opinion." I didn't immediately understand who he was referring to. My friend and I went out and asked at the reception, "Who is a gastroenterologist?" The receptionist smiled and said, "You don't know? A gastroenterologist is a stomach doctor."

As we were walking around the hospital, I noticed a sign outside a doctor's cabin that read "Nephrologist." My curiosity piqued, and I learned that a nephrologist is a kidney specialist. It turns out that every specialist has a specific medical term associated with their specialty. Today, using memory techniques, we'll learn how to remember the names of some of these specialist doctors.

Imagination Linking for Specialist Names

In this method, we give medical terms for doctors a reference image in our imagination, which is then linked to their actual meaning. For instance:

- ***Nephrologist*:** A kidney specialist. Imagine the word "nephro" sounds like "naphar" (which means hate in Hindi). Now, picture a kidney doctor who hates everyone.

- ***Gastroenterologist*:** A stomach specialist. Imagine the word "gastro" sounds like "gas." Picture yourself having severe gas in your stomach, so you go to see the stomach doctor.
- ***Cardiologist*:** A heart specialist. Imagine a "card" (like a wedding card) with a heart drawn on it, or a heart-shaped card.
- ***Orthopedician*:** A bone specialist. Imagine six women (ortho) in the hospital, putting plaster on broken bones.
- ***Neurologist**:** A brain specialist. Imagine a doctor performing brain surgery on a patient and finding a coconut (neuro) inside the brain.

These imaginative links will help you remember the specific medical terms associated with different specialist doctors.

Children's Doctor is Called a Pediatrician

Imagine that a children's doctor is climbing a tree (pedi-tree) to treat kids, or picture children getting hurt while climbing a tree, so they need to see a doctor. An ophthalmologist is an eye doctor. Imagine your friend's eyes are swollen due to an infection, and you say, "What a mess you've gotten yourself into! Let's quickly go to the doctor." This playful imagination will help you remember the medical terms.

So, if I ask, "What is a heart doctor called?" you'll recall the image of a heart on a card and remember that it's a cardiologist. Similarly, if I ask, "What is a children's doctor called?" you'll visualize kids climbing a tree and remember the word pediatrician.

Isn't it simple and effective?

❐

(31) Background Imagery Method

During our tenth-grade exams, a friend and I were returning home after a test. We were discussing the questions, and soon our discussion turned into a debate when we disagreed on the correct answer to one of the questions. I was absolutely confident that my answer was correct, while he was equally certain that his answer was right and mine was wrong. We ended up making a bet. Our curiosity and determination started to intensify as we defended our answers. When we got home, I quickly grabbed the book and looked up the answer. My friend looked at me, and I, in turn, closed the book with a thud. He smiled and asked, "So, what's the answer?" I handed him the book and said, "You won." His face lit up with the pride of a king who had just won a battle, while my face turned red like that of Maharaja Yudhishthira after losing a game of dice. Do you know why? Not because I lost the bet, but because I had mistakenly written the answer to a different question in place of the one I was supposed to answer. My friend, being a good sport, said, "No worries, buddy, it happens sometimes," and left. But I couldn't shake off the frustration, and a new question began to gnaw at my mind: Why and how did this happen, even after reading the material so many times? Why did my brain get confused, and what can be done to prevent this from happening again?

Background Imagery Method

Writing the answer to one question in place of another suggests that you had memorized the answers—otherwise, you wouldn't have been able to write anything at all. However, you only get marks if you write the correct answer in the correct place. So why does this confusion happen? The reason is often a mix-up due to similar content or common elements in the answers. For instance, suppose you need to discuss key points related to various countries, like the capital, currency, and parliament. For example, Japan's capital is Tokyo, its currency is the yen, and its parliament is the Diet. The confusing part here is that Japan is the common element in all three pieces of information, which can cause confusion about which currency or parliament belongs to which country.

To resolve this type of confusion, the Background Imagery Method proves to be effective. In this method, you assign a background image to the main and distinct aspects of the information. This image serves as a cue for the specific characteristic of the question. For instance, to remember the parliament, you could imagine a background image of the parliament building, and for the currency, you could visualize a bank.

For example, Japan's parliament is the Diet. Imagine standing in front of the parliament building and telling your friend, "Today, I'm on a diet, so I'll only eat betel leaves (paan)." Picture a paan shop in front of the parliament building selling special "diet" paan. You tell your friend, "Go bring Japan (pun intended)."

Similarly, when trying to remember the currency, imagine a background image of a bank. Japan's currency is the yen. Now, picture yourself in a bank with a van (yen sounds like 'yan') filled with paan (Japan). Visualize the van stuffed with paan, and you'll remember the yen. When there's no background image, logically you'll think of the capital.

Using the Background Imagery Method, you can eliminate confusion and reinforce your memory, making it easier to remember information accurately.

❐

32

Association Sentence Construction Method

The brain is like a computer's hard drive, with limitless capacity. However, the significance of a hard drive lies in the data it holds. For the brain, this data is memories. Memories can be of two types: temporary and permanent. Permanent memories are those that the brain never forgets, and any related information instantly comes to mind when prompted. On the other hand, temporary memories are often forgotten and do not come to mind immediately when needed. Interestingly, some things we deliberately try to remember, while others stick with us effortlessly. The memories that come to us naturally are often stronger than those we try hard to memorize.

For instance, when you were in school, you probably remember where the principal's office was, where you drank water, where you played, who sat next to you, and where the morning assembly was held. These memories are vivid even today, despite the fact that you never sat down to memorize them—they simply stayed with you. Similarly, when we watch a movie, we don't watch it with the intention of remembering it, yet it sticks with us. In contrast, despite our best efforts to memorize study material, it often doesn't stay with us for long. However, there's good news: any temporary memory can be converted into a permanent one, and the principle of association is particularly effective for this purpose.

Association Sentence Construction Method

This method helps us remember specific sequences or chronological orders. To use this technique, you create a sentence using the key words from the important information you need to remember. After that, you no longer need to repeatedly recall the entire subject matter; you only need to remember the sentence. The association principle makes it easy to recall this sentence naturally.

For example, take this peculiar sentence: "Clive wore Wallace's well-hazed bean doll, keen on light and ripe in car Ford, win wave, mount."

Memorize this odd sentence. You can also use visualization. Do you know what this sentence helps you remember? It encodes the chronological order of all the key Viceroys and Governors-General in history:

- Clive – Robert Clive
- War – Warren Hastings
- Wallace – Cornwallis
- Haze – Lord Hastings
- Bean – Lord Bentinck
- Doll – Lord Dalhousie
- Keen – Lord Canning
- Light – Lord Lytton
- Ripe – Lord Ripon
- Car – Lord Curzon
- Ford – Lord Chelmsford
- Win – Lord Irwin
- Wave – Lord Wavell
- Mount – Lord Mountbatten

Now, your brain has memorized all these important names in order. You can easily recall who came before or after whom with the help of this sentence. Instead of repeatedly reciting or memorizing all the names, you just need to remember this one sentence. You can create similar sentences to remember various subjects and questions using this method.

❐

(33)

Bizarre and Humorous Memory

Which is easier to remember: a joke or a theory? When I ask this question, everyone unanimously answers, "Jokes." Even if I tell you a joke you heard three years ago, you'll probably recognize it and remember how it ends. But when it comes to recalling what you read in a theory just three days ago, it's often a struggle. So why is this the case? After all, we read both jokes and theories. Why do jokes stick in our memory more quickly and for a longer time compared to theoretical content? Let's explore this.

Bizarre and Humorous Memory

Our brain pays attention to strange and unusual things. When something is out of the ordinary—whether it's weird, extraordinary, bizarre, or funny—the brain remembers it more quickly and retains it for a longer period. This is a unique feature of the brain.

For example, imagine you went to a fair and saw a twenty-foot-tall man. Later, when you think about the fair, what's the first thing that comes to mind? That twenty-foot-tall man, of course. Why? Because he was unusual, strange, and extraordinary. The brain has stored this as a special memory.

Now, imagine you attended a meeting with about thirty-five to forty people. Everyone introduced themselves: Ramesh, Suresh, Mohan, Ajay, Surendra, Ashish, Shalini, Dinesh, Rohit,

Rahul, and so on. Most of these names won't stick because, to the brain, they are ordinary pieces of information. But imagine if one of the attendees had a name like "Chapadganju" (a humorous, peculiar name). When you get home and someone asks who was at the meeting, you might say, "There were a lot of people, I don't remember everyone, but yes, there was someone named 'Chapadganju'." This name stands out because it's different, quirky, and funny, so the brain stores it as a special memory.

The point is that information that is unusual, funny, strange, different, extraordinary, or ridiculous is preserved by the brain as a special memory. This information is remembered more quickly and for a longer period. You can leverage this characteristic of the brain to help you remember study material. If you make your study content funny or bizarre, most of it will be easier to recall.

❒

(34)

Answer Method

Memory is formed by information, but how does the information stored in the brain come out? The trigger that brings this information from the brain into use is a question. As soon as a question is asked, the related information comes out from the brain. Every question has a direct connection to a memory of information; every answer is a retrieval of that memory. Life is essentially a process of questions and answers. Whether we're at home or outside, in school or with friends, whether we're talking to someone or even just to ourselves, we are either asking questions or providing answers. For example, "What are you doing?" "Where are you going?" "What's your name?" "Why did this happen?" Exams are full of questions, and your answers determine your results.

Today, let's understand how to approach answers in a way that ensures all the answers in life's exams are correct, leading to success.

Answer Method

For every question, the answer can either be right or wrong. Everyone wants to answer life's questions correctly and achieve success. Let's take a fresh perspective on the word "answer" so that our mind is trained to provide the right response to every question. The word "ANSWER" in English has the letters A, N, S, W, E, and R.

1. *A - Asking the Right Question*: First, ask yourself the right question: Why am I doing this task? When I was younger and studying, my sister would often turn on the TV in another room, and the sound would distract me. But when we read a newspaper or magazine on a moving train or bus, we can focus despite the noise around us. This means that external noise is not necessarily a distraction. The problem is that we often ask ourselves the wrong question. When we hear a noise, we might ask, "Why is this noise happening? Will I be able to study with this noise?" This question itself is wrong, leading to a negative answer. The right question should be, "Can any noise stop a determined champion like me from succeeding?" This shifts the focus from the noise to the goal, and the noise no longer bothers us.

2. *N - No to Worries*: Never stress. Whenever you do something, do it happily and stress-free. Stress reduces the brain's capacity to function effectively, while happiness and a positive mood enhance the brain's performance. Always tell yourself, "Nothing in this world can cause me stress. Everything is easy for me."

3. *S - Sleep*: Ensure you get seven to eight hours of good, sound sleep every day. A well-rested mind and body are healthy and full of energy and enthusiasm.

4. *W - Water*: Drink plenty of water. Water revitalizes the body and mind, and a refreshed mind is more successful. Drink one to two glasses of water after every hour of study.

5. *E - Emotions*: Information that we have an emotional connection with tends to become permanent. You remember your best friend's phone number, or childhood memories that had an emotional impact on you. Create an emotional connection with every question and its answer.

6. *R - Revision Plan*: Any information becomes permanent when it is revised regularly. Reviewing your subjects at least once a week helps you master them over time.

By viewing every answer through this lens, answering questions becomes easier, and the answers are more likely to be correct.

❐

(35)

Path Visualization Method

Welcome back to the brain gym.

The human brain uses the power of association to remember things. By linking information together, it forms memories. To quickly and effectively remember, we can use three-dimensional visualization.

Path Visualization Method

This method helps you remember directions. Often, we get lost on new routes, unable to recall when to turn left or right, leading us to ask for directions repeatedly. What should we do? Let's learn.

Imagine you are entering a new city in your car, and you need to reach your friend's house in Sarita Apartments, Sector 5. You ask someone for directions, and they guide you using landmarks:

"For Sector 5, go straight, take a left at the red light, then right after the hospital, another right at the post office, left at the big temple, take a U-turn in front of the school, then left after the police station. At the T-junction, turn right, go straight through the intersection, and under the overbridge, take a U-turn to reach Sector 5."

Sounds confusing, right? Let's make this complicated route easier to remember.

Any route consists of four main actions: Left, Right, Straight, and U-turn. In your imagination, assign a new meaning to each:

- *Left* becomes *Leaf* (pattiyaan)
- *Right* becomes *Red* (lal rang)
- *U-turn* becomes *Umbrella* (chhata)
- *Straight* remains as is (nothing to imagine).

Now, visualize the route:

1. *Go straight*, nothing to visualize here.
2. *Take a left at the red light* – Imagine placing leaves (pattiyaan) at the red light.
3. *Right after the hospital* – Visualize the entire hospital painted red (lal rang).
4. *Right at the post office* – Imagine the post office also painted red.
5. *Left at the temple* – Imagine leaves (pattiyaan) covering the temple.
6. *U-turn in front of the school* – Picture a huge umbrella (chhata) over the school.
7. *Left after the police station* – Visualize the police station filled with leaves (pattiyaan).
8. *Right at the T-junction* – Imagine painting the T-junction red.
9. *Straight through the intersection* – No visualization here, so you remember to go straight.
10. *U-turn under the overbridge* – Picture a big umbrella (chhata) on the overbridge.

As you encounter these landmarks on your journey, your imaginative cues will trigger the next direction. For example, when you see the temple, you'll recall the leaves and know to turn left. Isn't that amazing and easy?

❐

(36)

Harmony Phonetic Combination Method

Today, we will perform a unique experiment. Remembering square roots in mathematics can also be a challenging task. While square roots are calculated, there are some key square roots that need to be memorized because they are frequently used. For instance, the square root of ten is 3.161, eleven is 3.317, twelve is 3.464, thirteen is 3.605, fourteen is 3.741, fifteen is 3.873, and sixteen is 4. While remembering sixteen is easy, memorizing the others requires repeated effort. However, if we use two imagination techniques together, these can be easily remembered.

Harmony Phonetic Combination

Previously, we learned about the Harmony (Rhyme) and Phonetic methods. To recall, the Rhyme method involves creating a rhyming word for numbers based on their sounds and forming an image from it. For example, the main numbers are:

- Ten: Hen
- Eleven: Lemon
- Twelve: Shelf
- Thirteen: Fourteen: Fort in
- Fifteen: Lifting

For the Phonetic method, we use the letters corresponding to the numbers after the decimal point. Recalling the Phonetic method: Zero is S, One is T or D, Two is N, Three is M, Four is R, Five is L, Six is J or G, Seven is K, Eight is F or V, and Nine is P or B. By adding vowels to these symbols, we can create pictorial words. For instance:

For eleven's square root, which is 3.317: The rhyme for eleven is Lemon. For remembering the decimal part 3.317, we use common sense since 3.1 is common in square roots from ten to fifteen. The remaining 3.17 uses phonetic letters M, T, and K, so a word could be "Matka" (pot). Imagine lemons in a pot.

For fourteen's square root, which is 3.741: The rhyme for fourteen is "Fort in" (inside a fort), and the square root is 3.74. The phonetic letters are K, R, and T, so an image could be a "Cart" (vehicle) in a large fort.

If asked what the square root of eleven is, you would recall the rhyming image of Lemon and remember that lemons were in a pot. Decoding it, you get M, T, and K for 3.17, thus the answer would be 3.317.

You can use similar methods to remember other square roots or create your own.

❑❑❑

LEFT & RIGHT BRAIN : No Conflict but Synchronize

Brain is divided into two parts left brain and right brain and the functioning of both left brain and right brain are totally different.

In today's scenario, seeing the stress in learning, students often say -

Nothing is Left in Left Brain and Nothing is Right in Right Brain. Ha Ha, Jokes apart, the significant fact is that during a full life span an average human-being uses very little or a fraction of his brain potential, and mostly left brain, which signifies day to day activities like study, reading, calculation etc., It is a fact, and here I would like to have your attention and acknowledgment that your hardly use the right side of your brain, which is capable of creative activities like painting, associations, emotions, imagination, ideas and insights. Just question yourself right now. Isn't it right? Yes it is. Now further question, what will happen to your overall performance if you start using this very important right hand side of your brain? I bet you can increase your success rate and happiness manifolds and all the content in the ensuing pages will deal with this very significant aspect of your life. Neglecting one part of the mind will lead to poor performance. For an improved. Performance and super memory you should have a balanced and healthy mind.

The idea of left-brain and right-brain functions is often attributed to the research of neuro scientist Roger Sperry and his colleagues in the 1960s. Sperry conducted research on patients who had undergone surgery to sever the corpus callosum, which connects the left and right hemispheres of the brain. He found that these patients showed differences in cognitive abilities depending on which hemisphere of the brain was dominant for certain functions. However, it is important to note that the theory of distinct left-brain and right-brain functions has been challenged by more recent research suggesting that the two hemispheres of the brain work together in a more integrated way than previously thought.

The function of the left brain is to concentrate on Logics, Analysis, Sequencing, Linear, Mathematics, Language, Facts, Think in Words, Words of Songs, Computation. The significant fact is that during a full life span an average human being uses very little or a fraction of his brain potential, and mostly left brain, which signifies day to day activities like study, reading, calculation etc., It is a fact, and here I would like to have your attention and acknowledgment that your hardly use the right side of your brain, which is capable of creative activities like painting, associations, emotions, imagination, ideas and insights. Just question yourself right now. Isn't it right? Yes it is. Now further question, what will happen to your overall performance if you start using this very important right hand side of your brain? I bet you can increase your success rate and happiness manifolds and all the content in the ensuing pages will deal with this very significant aspect of your life.

Right Brain Function- Creativity, Though Right brain has functions like Creativity, Imagination, Holistic Thinking, Intuition, Arts (Motor Skill), Rhythm (Beats), Non-Verbal, Feelings, Visualization, Tune of Songs, Daydreaming, are the contents included in the right brain. But creativity has a significance. This is, anything which exists or does not exist, of which a human can think of and can create in real also. We can say that all the inventions done by so many people is the result of creativity. For example:- before creating an Airplane, Wright Brothers must have first created some picture in their mind and the ways of its execution and after that the plane was invented. So all these thinking is stored in the Right Brain. Imagination - According to 'Albert Einstein', *"Imagination is the most powerful thing in the world."* Imagination means watching images in your dream or in the mind which may not be in one's hand but is existing! All the images which one have ever seen or may not have seen exists in the right brain. For example: if just after listening the word 'Airplane' an image of it has been created is the work of Right Brain. Creativity works first and logic follows after, that means :

Logic Comes After and Imagination Comes First!

The significant fact is that during a full life span an average human being uses very little or a fraction of his brain potential, and mostly left brain, which signifies day to day activities like study, reading, calculation, etc. It is a fact, and here I would like to have your attention and acknowledgment that you hardly use the right side of your brain, which is capable of creative activities like painting, associations, emotions, imagination, ideas and insights. Just question yourself right now. Isn't it right? Yes it is. Now further question, what will happen to your overall performance if you start using this very important right hand side of your brain? I bet you can increase your success rate and happiness manifolds and all the content in the ensuing pages will deal with this very significant aspect of your life. Neglecting one part of the mind will lead to poor performance. For an improved performance and super memory you should have a balanced and healthy mind.

Left - Right Association for a Wonderful Memory

Some people make more use of left brain like scientists, mathematicians, etc. while some make more use of the right brain like writers, painters, musicians, etc. But the best way is keeping a balance between the left and the right brain. This lesson is all about the fluctuations, concentration and synchronization of brain. Sometimes left brain does not support the right brain and sometimes right brain does not support the left brain and brain science helps in the association of the left and right brain. This could be understood by a very simple example from day today life. Let us say once a mother told her two children named as Chintu and Mintu that today she'll be going out for shopping as tomorrow some guests are going to arrive at their place, so today I am giving you the responsibility to clean the house. If both of you will clean the house properly then I will give you chocolates and will allow you to play in the evening. So the mother distributed the work to both of them as the Chintu was told to clean the drawing room and the bedroom, and Mintu was told to clean the kitchen and the dining room, as, when the guests will arrive tomorrow the mother could say that this beautiful house has been decorated and cleaned by her children. They were bounded by the time limit of three hours. The children promises to do as the mother has said and then she leaves the house. After the mother left both of them got engaged in their respective works and after three hours when the mother arrived the house she was shocked to see the condition of the house as everything was badly messed up in the house, water was spilled all over the place, blankets were falling instead of being placed properly on the bed, table and chairs are some what broken.

In the kitchen water is splashed all over the place, vegetables are lying all over the floor, fridge has been kept open. In the drawing room the sofa set is out of place, all the things in the shelves are fallen down. In short, everything in the house was misplaced and destroyed because of which the mother gets extremely angry and calls both of them. They both arrives fighting with each other and the mother gives a slap on their faces and asks the reason behind the chaos. The mother scolds them and says I told you to clean the house in three hours and now the present condition of the house is so worse that it cannot be cleaned even in three days and also tomorrow the guests are arriving. They both started blaming each other. Chintu said that when Mintu cleaned the dining room he kept all the dust in the bedroom and Mintu said that he put all the dust in the kitchen after cleaning the drawing room. So now we can Say that as both of them were responsible for cleaning different things so for the sake of their own work they were trying to destroy the other's work because of which everything became complicated and everything was destroyed. And as a result the timing of the work increased from three hours to three days!! This happened because they had conflict between both of them and so they consumed their tie in two things one- completing their work and second- destroying others work. This also happens with our brain that when left and right brain both are in conflict and a work is given to the brain when it has to use both the sides than the synchronization gets disturbed.

Hence, this is what BRAIN SCIENCE teaches, the synchronization between left and right brain. Brain Science teaches different methods because of which the brain works on all three forms i.e. memorization, recollection, and retention.

Brain's Secret
'How to make permanent memory!'

Do you know, there are some factors by which you can keep your memory permanent or make any information permanent in your brain.

Our brain is like machine that checks through the important attributes in any information, the brain is receiving through senses.

First of all we should know that how many types of memory do we have or what types of information our brain receives!

Our brain receives any information through senses only.

Do you know how many senses do we have?

Most people say that we have five senses. But in brain science we can see,we have 7 senses. Commonly known senses are : Touch,Taste, Smell, Audio and Visual.

For touch sense we have skin. For smell, we have nose. For taste, we have tongue and mouth system. For audio, we have ear system. And for visual, we have eyes.

In brain science, we consider two more senses. Sixth sense and Common sense. Sixth sense, is the intuition sense, in which you sense through your intuition and inner voice. Scientists say and accept, that we do have sixth sense and we do have intuition by which we can predict about the information.

And, 7th sense is Common Sense or logical sense by which, we understand about the information conceptually and we process the information logically.

Logical sense is popularly known as common sense.

Our brain receives information through the senses and processes.

Then brain makes these information as a memory.

We can train our all senses along with logical or common sense, through a popular brain training and a proper practice.

In humans, the dominating sense is visual and other senses are supporting senses to make any memory.

To remember anything and to retain longer, we should create a visual or picture while storing them in brain.

Brain science techniques can become a very useful tool and a very big help to do the same.

Now we talk about, how to keep our memory permanent.

I am now going to tell you the factors by which you can keep your memory as permanent and you can convert any memory into permanent memory

Our brain has a scanning and checking system, when brain receives any information through senses, brain tries to find six factors in that information.

These factors are:

1. Interest
2. Emotion
3. Visual
4. Association
5. Creativity and
6. Logic

These are 6 factors by which the brain can understand that, this memory will be a permanent memory.

If any information has all these factors, then that will become a permanent memory automatically. Any information which has as many factors of these factors, will be permanent memory more likely.

Let us understand this with examples one by one.

1. Interest: The things we are interested in or the information which is interesting in nature, is more likely to be a longer and stronger memory.

Some people may have interest in politics, some kids may have interest in video games, some people may have interest in Bollywood, some people have interest in cricket. You can see that the people who are interested in any field, they have a better memory about the same field also.

If we have the information which has the interest factor at higher level, will become a permanent memory or a long time memory.

2. Emotion: Any information that changes our emotion or that has a big impact on our emotion, can be a permanent memory. Have you noticed, that many things we have read just two days before we are not able to recall but so many things which we did not revise or recall and which is very very old memory like of our childhood even,we can recollect today easily. That old memory is recollected without revision for lifetime why, because that is attached with our emotions. Another amazing fact is, of how many people do you remember the phone numbers! Yours and apart from you, of whom, you remember the phone number that is the person you are emotionally attached with. Yes or no! So if you can put emotion in any information while receiving your brain will make this information important and permanent.

3. Visual: As I already told you that visual sense is our dominating sense.

Most things you remember for long time are visual and incidents. We do not remember a book which has only texts but we usually remember the book which has many pictures. Be more precise, you do not remember the text but we remember the movie. We watch the movie and usually most part of the movie we can remember. Movie was created from a script which was text when Written, finally it became a video and a visual and that's why the movie is usually remembered for long time.

4. Association: In psychology, there is a factor to keep memory permanent and to remember the things for long time, is called as Association.

Association is the process by which a brain can remember most information which are linked together. Your brain is like your home. At home what are the things which are lost usually, have you noticed?

Although many things which are visual or we can see them still we forget where we have kept them.

Like it happens where is my pen, my book is missing, where are the keys lost and where are socks, or the important documents.

My handkerchief is missing my wallet is missing. These problems, we experience, at home many times.

But have you ever heard that the tomatoes are missing and the lemons are not being able to be found. No because you have kept them at a certain place, and that place is known as refrigerator.

Refrigerator here becomes the logical association to keep the things which are edibles. Because of the refrigerator the edible things are found easily and you do not forget them. So this is an association by which you can link two things or information together and because of the one thing, second thing will not be lost because it is linked.

5. Creativity: Where we use our creativity and we create the new things and we make anything mostly when our creativity is used the information becomes a permanent memory. Scientist remember their inventions and theories, painters know their paintings, poets mostly remember their poetry. Even a kid who is playing video game they remember all the stages and all the parts of that game. Because they are using their creativity.

It is a very important factor to make an important memory and to keep that memory permanent for brain. Human is a creative creature.

6. Logic: Our brain remembers the things which are logical in nature when brain understands the logic or the concept behind the information brain keeps the information as permanent or for a long time. Like mathematics is a logical subject. Once you learn how to add or subtract or divide or multiply or derive any percentage, you can do it for lifetime. This logical memory becomes your permanent memory because it has a factor that is called as logic. Therefore in most education systems the focus is on the more logical development of a child. Conceptual and logical clarity has more importance. Science is also a logical and conceptual subject. Logic gives us a sense of belief also, we believe on the things or information, of which, we are clear about the logic behind, when we say that this is scientific that means we know that it has a logical and science, so, this is believable.

My dear readers, in this chapter we have understood that how we can keep the things permanent in our brain if we put all these factors while making any memory from the information. The irony is in education when students need to remember more or memorize many things they do not have these factors in their educational content. When a child is studying in their study content usually children do not find more interest and children are least or less interested in studying over the other things. Whereas, the children are more interested in their games or videos or movies or their other personal things.

Children are not emotional towards their studies and the subject content while they are more emotional in other things in their personal life.

Study content is more of a text than visual, that is the reason, the children become bored when they are studying very easily.

Children neither use their creativity in studies while they use their own creativity in their personal interests like games, video games and other things, nor they know how to use Association while studying.

These are the main reasons why students tend to forget their subjects and study content when they study while they need to remember the study for long so, that need is important but the process is weak. Students need to learn brain science if they really want to make their study permanent in brain.

By adding these factors in the information or if we can create the information along with these factors so the brain can understand, that, this information has all the factors to keep it permanent, we can remember forever.

So, with these Memory Tricks

TRAIN YOUR BRAIN

THANKS